J.JOI
AND CHRIS W

What does
GOD
want of us?

British Library Cataloguing in Publication Data

A catalogue record for this book is available from the British Library

ISBN: 978-0-9573890-3-8

Cover design by Rachel Fung

Print Management by Verité CM Ltd

Printed in England

CONTENTS

LEARNING TO WALK WITH GOD

CONTINUING TO WALK WITH GOD

INTRODUCTION

Around 2,750 years ago, a prophet called Micah addressed a question to a society that had lost its way. 'What does God want of us?' he asked and – in the next breath – he gave the answer: 'To act justly and to love kindness and to walk humbly with your God.' This passage, which you can find in Micah 6:8, raises the biggest of questions: 'What does God want of us?' It follows up with an appropriately big answer.

At first glance the three parts of this answer seem to be three commands: *act justly* (that is, do right actions), *love kindness* (have right attitudes) and, finally, *walk with your God*. In fact, the best way of understanding this is to see the first two statements as commands that set out the nature of the right way. The last statement, 'walk humbly with your God,' however, is something else: it is the great summary of *how* we can walk the right way. Life is often thought of in terms of a journey or a road that must be travelled. Yet the road of life is more of an obstacle course than a straight path for most of us. This book is about seeking God's will for our lives. But it is not a set of lectures about the nature of the road of life, where it goes and why it is where it is. Instead, it is a practical guidebook about how to seek the right way and how to walk it with God – how to find out what God wants of us and then to act upon it.

Micah's question and answer is a thread that runs through this book. The first part of the book is about finding the way and working out what it means to carry out right actions and have right attitudes. The second part is about having God as guide along the way. The third part covers the practical issues of continuing the walk with God.

Two points before we begin. First, if you look at Micah 6:8 in a Bible, you will almost certainly find something slightly different to this translation – 'to act justly and to love kindness and to walk humbly with your God'. While the overall sense of the original Hebrew is clear, putting it into English isn't easy and the versions differ. After a lot of thought, study and discussion, we have made our own translation which seems to us to best reflect the meaning of the text. Second, there are enormous depths to this verse. In a way it summarises the entire message of the Old Testament, if not the Bible. A whole book could be written about this verse but our aim is to take the three statements mentioned in the passage: the 'acting justly', the 'loving kindness' and the 'walking humbly with God' and apply them directly to our lives. So let's begin.

WALKING **THE RIGHT WAY**

'What does God want of us?' Micah asked. The answer he gave was, 'To act justly and to love kindness and to walk humbly with your God.'

What is the right way in life? This verse spells it out. It is to act justly and to love kindness: to live according to right actions and right attitudes. Although there is no fixed boundary between actions and attitudes, nevertheless it makes sense to treat these two areas of our lives separately. In this part, we will look at what it means both 'to act justly' and 'to love kindness'. Let's begin with right actions.

CARRYING OUT RIGHT ACTIONS: 1
THE NEED TO ACT

What does God want of us? To act justly and to love kindness and to walk humbly with your God. The first thing God requires, says Micah, is for us to 'act justly'. It would be easy to instantly leap to that word 'justly' and begin to think about what it means. But to do that would be to overlook something more basic but very important – we need to act.

Life is a continuous series of choices. Every day, from waking to sleeping, we make a vast number of decisions. Some are trivial: What colour sweater do I wear? Do I have a coffee or a tea? Do I watch TV or a DVD? Some of them are serious: Do I accept that job offer? Do I buy that new car? Do I move house? Some of these decisions are made quickly or instinctively and others are made after careful consideration and consultation. It is not just actions that we decide about either – we also have to decide what to say. We tend to think of words as being less important than actions – yet words can comfort, encourage, inspire and injure as much as any actions. We must decide not only about what we do, but also what we say.

We can see the different areas where we must make decisions as being a series of concentric zones. The innermost zone of our lives centres on us as individuals. We all have to face decisions about what sort of people we are and what priorities we have. Are we going to be people who think others are important or are we going to put ourselves, our possessions or our reputation first? Then, going outward, there is the zone of our home or family life. Here we face endless decisions about how we are to treat our spouses, our children, our parents, our other relatives and how we spend our time and our money. For many of us the next zone out is our workplace. Do we decide to work hard or simply aim to get away with the minimum needed? Do we choose to be honest or dishonest? Do we live for work or do we work to live? Another zone is that of our community. Here we must choose whether to be involved or not. Do we work at helping neighbours or do we ignore them and live in isolation? Yet our decisions about how we act do not stop here. At the level of our nation there are issues that cry out for action and involvement. We may cast our vote at election time, yet there is so much more that we can and ought to do.

The final zone where we need to make decisions is that of our world. It is tempting to think that we can do very little whereas, merely by living in one of the world's most prosperous countries, we do have an effect globally. But we can – and should – go further to change our world for the better. After observing Mother Teresa's work among the poor in Calcutta a reporter commented to her that what she was doing was just 'a drop in the ocean'. 'Ah yes,' she replied, 'but the ocean is made of drops.' In fact, history shows that determined individuals can make an enormous difference to the world.

So we all have to make decisions about our priorities and what actions we will take. Yet the question of how we are to act is made harder by two things. First of all, actions (and words) can change and affect our lives. Some decisions are momentous. So, for instance, the choice of whether or not to go on to further education is often life-changing. You know that, looking at your life in ten, twenty or fifty years' time, you will see your decision as a crossroads.

The second thing that increases the problem of how to act is that once actions are undertaken, they may not be reversible. Imagine you are typing something on a computer – it is easy to change what you have written, delete some words and restore others until you have got what you want. But life is more like writing a letter with pen and ink and with no clean sheet of paper if you mess up. In life, many of our actions cannot be undone: all too frequently we find that we cannot retrace our steps. Even words once spoken can never be withdrawn. Now, of course, we can – and do – get second chances. But second chances are like the airbags and seat belts in cars: it is best not to proceed along the road of life in such a way as to make their use inevitable!

It is precisely because actions are so momentous and can be so permanent that many people fall into a subtle temptation: they decide not to act at all. You hear them say, 'I'll let things take their course' or 'Let's see what happens.' Unfortunately, to decide not to act is actually to take a decision in itself. And not to act is sometimes a very unwise decision. Think, for instance, of parents who decide that they don't want to discipline a misbehaving child but choose instead 'to let things go'. The long-term consequences for both parents and child are likely to be miserable. Furthermore, in some situations both the law and public opinion can consider a failure to act as a guilty action. If we choose not to act, we can only blame ourselves if things end up badly wrong in our family, our workplace or even our country. There is a quote attributed to an eighteenth-century writer, Edmund Burke, that 'all that is needed for evil to triumph is for good men to do nothing'. In the light of the events of the two hundred years since those words were spoken, all we would want to add to his statement today is to make it gender-inclusive. As the US president Theodore Roosevelt said, 'In any moment of decision the best thing you can do is the right thing, the next best thing is the wrong thing, and the worst thing you can do is nothing.'

Part of being human is that we are given responsibility to act, and that responsibility is both a blessing and a curse. Quite frequently, to stand by and just do nothing is to do the worst thing. Strange to say, the first step in 'acting justly' may be to act.

Two final comments. First, it is easy for us to give the impression – by generating a flood of words or deeds – that we really are doing something. The person who pauses, thinks and then quietly does a single action may be doing far more than someone who is a whirlwind of noise and gestures. As the writer Ernest Hemingway said, 'Never mistake motion for action.' Second, there is an incidental benefit to taking action. People who don't take action often spend their lives making sure that no one else does either. Whether in families or businesses, a lot of people find that they are more preoccupied with squabbling over why they are going nowhere than with actually going anywhere. Taking action focuses our energies away from ourselves towards the task in hand. If you want to walk the right way, the very first thing to do is to decide to walk.

CARRYING OUT RIGHT ACTIONS: 2
THE NEED TO ACT JUSTLY

In order to walk the right way, it is not enough to drift – we need to take action. But what sort of action? What should we do? Micah sets down the first guideline here – the right way involves us acting *justly*. What does that mean? It means to act in a way that is right, fair and impartial; to act with justice. It is to do the right thing, in the right way, with the right motives. The traditional image of justice is helpful. Justice is represented as being a blindfolded woman with scales and a sword – her scales are to weigh matters, her sword is to carry out judgement and her blindfold is to show that she is absolutely neutral. She can be trusted to be fair.

Sometimes it is easy to see what something really is by looking at what it is not. So darkness can be defined as the absence of light and peace as the absence of conflict. And similarly what it is to 'act justly' can be seen by thinking about what it is to act unjustly. From the book of Micah we learn that his society was one in which injustice flourished. Money had become more important than morality, the powerful had stolen the land that belonged to the weak, false weights and measures were widely used in the marketplace, and lying was widespread. The people responsible for enforcing justice – the judges – benefited from the abuses of power. And the very people who should have publicly criticised the legal corruption, the religious leaders, ignored what was happening for the same reason. In a society that was supposed to be based upon a God-given pattern of social justice, the level of unfairness was appalling.

For all the technological and cultural developments that have occurred since Micah's day, our own world is not so different. Much is done in public and private that is both unfair and unjust. While injustice in Britain may not yet have reached the spectacular levels seen in many countries, it is still present throughout the fabric of our society and its structures. So a man gets preferential treatment by the legal system because he can afford an influential lawyer. A woman manages to jump a hospital waiting list because she has 'connections'. Someone else is awarded a large salary increase while at the same time making hundreds redundant. And still another person avoids employing the best candidate for a job because she is prejudiced against him because of his gender or race.

Injustice occurs at every level of life; it is to be found between individuals and between nations. In a marriage, someone may accuse their spouse of something – perhaps overspending, laziness or untidiness – that they permit in themselves. And, at the international level, a poor country may find that whatever profits they make constantly vanish in a futile attempt to pay interest on debts that never decrease. Both are unfair and both represent injustice – the only difference is one of scale.

Acting justly is hard because it means considering other people's needs and letting our own preferences and interests be pushed to one side. There is always a tendency to put ourselves first, whatever the cost for other people. We are all in favour of the triumph of justice as long as it rules in our favour. In fact, the whole idea of acting with justice is neglected today because justice, or even simply 'doing the right thing', is no longer the main rule of how we are to live. For most people today the ruling principle of life is that of personal pleasure: everything focuses on *me, I* and *myself*. We are encouraged to assess everything on the basis of whether or not it benefits us personally. Yet acting justly is one of the great rules of doing what God wants and to act unjustly is to start to head off on the wrong path.

In fact, acting justly is not simply good for us, it is good for those around us. To act unjustly is often to start a chain reaction of injustice, a vicious spiral that ends up in destruction all round. Sadly, injustice is contagious. There is a story about a baker who came to suspect that the farmer from whom he bought his butter was cheating him. So for an entire week he carefully weighed the butter and, sure enough, his suspicions were confirmed. Irate, he had the farmer arrested. At the hearing, the judge asked the farmer: 'I assume you use standard weights when measuring your goods?'

'As a matter of fact I don't,' responded the farmer.

'Well then, how do you do your measuring?'

'You see, your honour, when the baker began buying butter from me, I decided to buy his bread, and I measure out his butter by placing his one-pound loaf of bread on the other side of the scale.'

Justice is also vital for our society. An unjust society breeds injustice and further wrongs. It encourages anger and bitterness, and where there is no justice people take the law into their own hands. To work to build a just society is not simply to engage in naïve and wishful thinking, it is to be wise. Societies that are based on justice are strong and stable. To seek a just society may also be a shrewd move – no one, not even the most powerful in the land, can tell when the wheel may turn and they may need justice for themselves. Unjust societies are always weak, fragile and generally short-lived; injustice is the ideal breeding ground for violence and rebellion. As Francis Bacon said in the seventeenth century, 'If we do not maintain justice, justice will not maintain us.'

So at every level, whether at home, in society, in our nation or globally, we need to act justly. But what *exactly* does it mean to 'act justly'? In Micah's day, his contemporaries would have understood exactly what he meant and what he was expecting from them. They would have thought about the solemn covenant between them and God and would have known that they, in turn, had to keep the rules and commandments that were their side of that arrangement. They knew what they had to do. We do not; we live in a different world. So what standards or guidelines are we to measure ourselves against when we consider what it is to act justly?

Some people argue that every society and culture today has a different view of what is right and wrong so that expressions such as 'justice' or 'right and wrong' have no fixed, absolute meaning. The result is that such people say confidently, 'You have your code of morality and I have mine; both are as valid (or invalid) as each other, because there is no absolute standard.' Such an attitude undermines any plea for people to 'act justly' because it denies that there is any real standard of justice. There are, however, all sorts of problems in taking such a view. For instance, there must be a strong suspicion that those who declare in public that there is no such thing as 'good' or 'bad' or 'right' or 'wrong' tend to adopt a more traditional view when they find that their house has been burgled or that their best friend has run off with their spouse. Certainly, the idea that there is no such thing as absolute right or wrong is not held popularly. If it were, then we might as well close our prisons because every accused person would plead that they were 'acting justly' according to their own moral standards. 'I find myself not guilty,' they could say in court, 'and my standards are just as valid as those of society.'

The fact is that we all have some standard against which we measure ourselves. The eighteenth-century philosopher Voltaire said, 'The sentiment of justice is so natural, and so universally acquired by all mankind, that it seems to be independent of all law, all party, all religion.' If it is necessary to 'act justly' in order to do what God wants of us, then we urgently need some sort of guidelines as to what justice really is. In fact, there are three great standards for how we should live. You can think of these standards either as rules that we must obey (as if they were the Highway Code of the way of life) or as signposts to the right way to live. The reality is that they serve both functions: they both judge *and* guide us. So let's look at the first standard.

THE FIRST STANDARD OF THE RIGHT WAY TO LIVE:
THE INBUILT MORAL CODE

The first standard of how we are to go along the way of life is the general moral code that seems to be present in all human beings. It is the sense of what is right or wrong that is so universal that it may very well be written into the genetic code of *Homo sapiens.* It is the standard that – even if they do not keep it – everyone, everywhere approves of. You can see that such a universal moral code exists by the fact that people across the world, from every sort of racial, cultural and educational background, have similar reactions when faced with issues of right and wrong. So, for instance, every human society values courage over cowardice, honesty over deception, loyalty over treachery and generosity over selfishness. In every culture, crime, greed, lawlessness and immorality are condemned.

The existence of this universal moral code can be seen by looking at what cultures value. Take, for example, films. Many films have had global success and have appealed to men and women across different cultures. Very many of these films are based on moral issues such as the victory of good over evil, the fight against tyranny or the worth of each human life. Their global success suggests that the values on which the films are based are appreciated and understood worldwide. Even if the words need subtitles, the values around which the plots are based need no explanation; there is no confusion about who is the hero and who is the villain.

You can see further evidence that humanity has an inbuilt moral code in the existence of such organisations as the United Nations, the establishment of which required a consensus that peace, justice, prosperity and freedom were good and that war, injustice, poverty and oppression were bad. There are shared values.

Of course, there are differences in how this universal moral code is applied. Some societies may allow a man to marry only one woman, while in others he may marry two or more. Nevertheless, there is still some sort of moral code there. So no society approves of a situation where a man can take whatever woman he desires whether she is married or not. While some societies may allow theft, they tend to consider it only permissible as long as it is not from someone within the family. In other societies, family or personal honour may have come to take precedence over absolute right and wrong. You might think that such apparently immoral bodies as Mafia gangs, or societies that have fragmented during bloody civil wars, disprove any sense of an inbuilt morality. Yet such groups do turn out to have a morality, it's just that they limit the extent of honesty, forgiveness and charity to their own clan or family. They have a morality; they just don't share it too widely! And, of course, in every society there are people who have deliberately chosen to ignore this universal moral code.

How can we sum up this moral code? Jesus summarised what we might call the universal principle of justice like this: 'So in everything, do to others what you would have them do to you, for this sums up the Law and the Prophets' (Matthew 7:12, NIV). This statement is often called 'The Golden Rule'. Here Jesus is giving – in its purest and most refined form – what is more or less universally recognised. In fact, almost every religion in the world has some belief like this. Whenever you hear a teacher or parent saying to a bullying child, 'And how would you like it if they did that to you?' you hear the Golden Rule being taught again.

Christians view this inbuilt and universal standard of morality, the conscience, as the result of human beings being made in the image of God. Deep inside every human being is something, some mental circuitry, which lays down this most basic rule of behaviour. Of course, the conscience is not always obeyed. People can distort it or even overrule it altogether. But we know it is there and therefore all of us know, more or less, what it is to 'act justly'. Yet all of us also know – if we are honest – that, however much we struggle, we will never manage to keep totally even this most basic of guidelines.

Despite its widespread nature, however, this universal standard of morality is simply the lowest common denominator of how we try to live out our lives. Conscience may be known by everyone (even if they ignore it) but it is a vague and imprecise standard. It is the first step – but we need to go further.

THE SECOND STANDARD OF THE RIGHT WAY TO LIVE: **THE TEN RULES**

The first standard or signpost of the right way to live is the general and universal moral code, the inbuilt sense of right and wrong that all people have. The good news is that it is universal – the bad news is that it is very limited. The second standard of behaviour is much more specific – it is that of the Ten Commandments that are listed in the Bible (Exodus 20:1–17). These ancient laws lie at the basis of Jewish faith and were taken up by Christianity; Jesus referred to them and gave his own interpretation of many of them. They have formed the basis of Western civilisation and are respected in Islam.

There is a lot that could be said about the Ten Commandments and one of us (J.John) has covered them at much greater length, both in a book (*Ten: Living the Ten Commandments in the 21st Century*) and in a video series; many more details and applications can be found there (see Appendix). Here, though, we simply want to give a brief summary of what each commandment says and what it means.

However, before we look at the Ten Commandments, we need to realise that they were not just given in a vacuum, as if God shouted them out to the first tribe who happened to be passing Mount Sinai. They have a context and that is that they are part of the covenant – the binding agreement – between God and his people. God had already, out of love, chosen his people and rescued them and the commandments are part of the covenant agreement that put this relationship on a formal and permanent basis.

The Ten Commandments, then, are not some sort of moral ultimatum, as if God was a dictator ('Do this or else!'). Instead, they are what God considers to be the right response of his family to his kindness and covenant love. One way of thinking about the commandments is to imagine a child who is rescued out of dreadful circumstances and adopted into a wonderful, loving family. Once the child is settled in, their new parents tell them what the 'rules' of the household are. 'These,' they say, 'are about how we do things here.' And that is what the Ten Commandments are about: they are the directions about what is appropriate for those who are in God's family.

Let's look briefly at the Ten Commandments. They start with how we are to relate to God and then move to how we are to relate to other people.

1. 'DO NOT WORSHIP ANY OTHER GODS BESIDES ME'

'You have been rescued by me,' says God, 'I expect your undivided loyalty.' This commandment is a ruling against the universal temptation for us to hedge our bets, to back one God against another or to try to seek better terms elsewhere. This commandment rules that only the one true God is to be worshipped.

2. 'DO NOT MAKE IDOLS OF ANY KIND'

If the first commandment says that we must worship the right God, the second says that we must worship him in the right way. The fact is that any attempt to portray or represent God, even with the best motives, will inevitably mislead us by reducing who God really is. If we bring God down to our level we are no longer treating him as God. We must remember that our imaginations as well as our hands can make idols.

3. 'DO NOT MISUSE THE NAME OF THE LORD YOUR GOD'

The third commandment prohibits distorting who God is by what we say. This commandment isn't just a prohibition of blasphemous swearing – it is a prohibition of the careless abuse of God's character. This commandment is meant to stop us saying things that are misleading about God. It is also meant to ensure that we avoid using God's name as a way of recklessly boosting our promises or our threats.

4. 'KEEP THE SABBATH DAY HOLY'

The Sabbath day was one day a week set aside for rest and dedication to God. Its purpose centres on time, and how we use it. We tend to think of time as being our own. Yet it is not; time is a gift of God and he gives it and takes it away as he sees fit. As a reminder of that fact, God's covenant people are told to devote a day a week to him and to make that day separate from other days. The Sabbath was also to be a weekly reminder to God's people that they were in a special relationship with him.

5. 'HONOUR YOUR FATHER AND MOTHER'

With the fifth commandment there is a switch in emphasis. Up until now the commandments have been about our dealings with God – they now shift to cover how we deal with each other. Here the specific rule for God's people is that they must respect and honour their parents. Implied in this commandment is a respect for the structure of the family generally.

6. 'DO NOT MURDER'

Life is a gift from God and there should be no unauthorised taking of life, whether intended (as in murder) or unintended (as in manslaughter). It is plain from the context, and from elsewhere in the Old Testament, that this commandment does not prohibit either capital punishment or killing in warfare and the issues these raise are not addressed here. Behind this commandment lies the belief that people are made in the image of God. As such, human beings are sacred and to murder someone is to injure God himself.

7. 'DO NOT COMMIT ADULTERY'

Not only is human life sacred but so is the marriage relationship. As laid down early in the Bible (see Genesis 2:24) men and women were made by God to be united physically only in the specific context of the social, legal and spiritual union that is marriage. A marriage relationship is therefore to be honoured and protected by all. Implied in the condemnation of adultery is also a rejection of anything that undermines marriage. For God's people, their covenant commit-ment to each other in marriage is to be a small-scale version of God's covenant commitment to them: it is to be unbreakable.

8. 'DO NOT STEAL'

God wants people to have respect not only for the lives and marriages of others but also for their property. The strong cannot simply take what they want from the weak. Theft, though, can involve more than money – you can steal by robbing people of their rights, their freedom, their dignity and their reputation.

9. 'DO NOT TESTIFY FALSELY AGAINST YOUR NEIGHBOUR'

In the ninth commandment the focus shifts from actions to words: God's people are not to use false words with each other. The word 'neighbour' here really means whoever we come in contact with. While this prohibition against false testimony refers primarily to words in law courts, it also applies more generally; it is wrong to spread harmful untruths about other people under any circumstances.

10. 'DO NOT COVET ANYTHING THAT BELONGS TO OTHERS'

This final commandment states that we are not to desire what is not ours. The details – 'You must not covet your neighbour's house. You must not covet your neighbour's wife, male or female servant, ox or donkey, or anything else that belongs to your neighbour' – may sound archaic (or even sexist) today, but the point is plain. Whatever belongs to someone else is not for the taking; it is not even for the desiring. This commandment is concerned exclusively with our thought life, and demonstrates that attitudes cannot be separated from actions. In prohibiting coveting, the tenth commandment attacks the wrong desires that are the very root of all wrong activities.

The Ten Commandments are barely 300 words long in English and a mere 120 words in the original Hebrew.

When you think of all the libraries of law books, it is amazing how wide a span the Ten Commandments covers. Family rights, property rights, the rights of the individual and even God's rights are all included here.

Despite their antiquity, these rules retain an incredible relevance today. Even at the most basic psychological, sociological and medical level, they make extraordinarily good sense. After all, what better recipe for personal happiness can there be to (a) take a day off work every week, (b) live in harmony with your family, (c) avoid murder, (d) stay faithful to your spouse, (e) never steal, (f) never lie and (g) avoid greed?

It is significant that, despite three thousand years of persistent effort, no one has come up with a real alternative to the Ten Commandments. All that tends to happen is that bits get removed. So atheists remove Numbers One to Four, adulterers ditch Number Seven and advertisers marginalise Number Ten. But no alternative proposal has won any sort of acceptance. What tends to happen is that the commandments get treated as God's 'Ten Suggestions'. But they were not given to be taken on an optional or a 'pick-and-mix' basis. They remain *commandments*.

THE THIRD STANDARD OF THE RIGHT WAY TO LIVE:
THE ONE PERFECT LIFE

So far, we have looked at two standards or signposts that give us directions to the right way of life. We started with the idea of a universal moral code, a standard that – although vague and imprecise – was held by all people everywhere. The second standard – that of the Ten Commandments – is more helpful because it is more specific.

But are the Ten Commandments adequate as a signpost and standard for us to walk the right way? Do they point the way sufficiently for us to need nothing more? The answer is no. For all their greatness, the Ten Commandments are not enough. First, although they condemn wrong deeds and thoughts, they are essentially negative; in them we learn what we ought *not* to do, but not what we ought to be. Second, although far more specific than any version of the Golden Rule, the Ten Commandments remain only general principles. Third, the Ten Commandments are powerless. They condemn us, but they do not provide us with help. Like the tablets of stone that they are, they weigh us down and do nothing to lift us up. They are guidance but they are not a *guide*.

The Ten Commandments enormously clarify the vague and general standards of the inbuilt moral code. Nevertheless, we need what might be called the ultimate standard – Jesus. It would take more than another book to explore adequately who Jesus is; here we just want to mention the three ways in which Jesus is a standard or signpost to how we are to live. But before we do that, it is important to emphasise that Jesus cannot be simply dismissed as some mythological figure or the invention of early Christianity. What we know about Jesus we know primarily from the four Gospels (Matthew, Mark, Luke and John) and also from the many references to him in the other books of the New Testament. These accounts all treat Jesus as a real person and there is no hint of him being a myth. Some people have assumed that what happened was that a 'Jesus Myth' grew up; that increasingly wonderful legends grew up about someone who had, in reality, been no more than a remarkable Jewish preacher. However, there is good evidence that some, if not all, the Gospels were written no later than forty years after Jesus' death – something that hardly gives time for such legends to emerge. For another, we know from the New Testament letters, which can be accurately dated, that within twenty years of his crucifixion, Jesus was already being thought of by his followers in much the same way as he is by Christians today. They believed that he was somehow God in human form, that he had been raised from the dead and that he was going to return at the end of the world. Such extraordinary beliefs so soon after his death suggest that he is indeed much more than an extraordinary man. Jesus is a standard or signpost to how we are to live, in three ways.

1. JESUS IS ONE OF US

In terms of Jesus' background and social level, he lived in the relative poverty where most of our world has always lived. There is no indication that he was anything other than ordinary in his person or manner – none of the Gospel accounts of his life tell us what he looked like. He was familiar with ordinary things and knew family, friends, festivities, joy and humour. He also knew hard work, solitude, pain, hunger and tiredness and, finally, ridicule, injustice, torture and a brutal death. If you could plot everything that human beings are, then Jesus would be in the middle of it all. It is as if Jesus came to be the human being we could all identify with.

2. JESUS IS DIFFERENT TO US

Yet if Jesus was, in every way, an ordinary human being, there is something extraordinary about him. Even if you take the accounts of Jesus' life in the Gospels simply as reasonably accurate records of what he did and said, a remarkably consistent picture emerges of an extraordinary man without equal either before or since. Consider the following:

- Jesus made staggering claims about himself, yet was deeply humble. The focus of his teaching was that people should follow him, and he put himself above all the prophets, kings and leaders of the past. He claimed that he personally would judge the world. Yet at the same time, he claimed to be humble and gentle and to be the servant of all – and his actions showed that this humility was genuinely lived out.

- Jesus proposed the highest possible moral standards and then – astonishingly – kept them. Even his enemies made no accusation of immorality or wrongdoing against him. It is an almost universal truth that preachers of morals have double standards – they teach 'Do as I say; don't do as I do.' But Jesus was different; he walked the talk.

- Jesus' teaching showed a remarkable independence from pressure or persuasion. Whether being wooed by the rich, bullied by the powerful or acclaimed by the people, he did not alter his message. Leaders often yield to praise or pressure, yet Jesus stayed unaffected by both.

- In a world where oppression is invariably met by hatred, Jesus never retaliated. Although sensitive to injustice, Jesus never – even on the cross – resorted to rage or bitterness against those who persecuted him.

- Sadly, the most subtle trap for spiritual people is that they get stifled by 'religion'. They start off as prophets and end up trapped in ritual, rules and religious bureaucracy. Yet Jesus remained unaffected by the pressures to 'be religious'.

- The accounts of Jesus' miracles show a remarkable consistency with his teaching. Jesus made claims to be divine, to be the Lord of nature, to be able to forgive sins, to know God the Father personally and to have overcome spiritual evil. The miracles were visual aids to demonstrate that he was indeed all these things. The ultimate proof of these claims came in his own resurrection.

In summary, the picture of Jesus given in the Gospels is astonishing. It is either a depiction of the most extraordinary human being ever to walk the earth or the most extraordinary fictional achievement of human imagination. Most people who have given the matter serious thought have concluded that the first possibility is far more likely than the second.

3. JESUS IS A PATTERN FOR US

Jesus, then, is one of *our* kind, but he is also one of *a* kind. How do we explain the fact that he is both similar and different to us? Part of the answer is that, in him, God is showing us how our lives ought to be. In Jesus, we see the third standard – the ultimate direction sign – made flesh and blood.

Once there was a multinational firm with a subsidiary factory that was a long way away. This factory was instructed to manufacture some complex items and the plans and technical drawings were sent out to them. The results, however, were a failure; quite simply the machines didn't work properly. In fact, some of the production engineers in the factory began to doubt that properly functioning machines could ever be built. Finally, the head office sent them an actual model: a sample of what the product ought to be.

In some ways, Jesus is like that. It is as if, when we look at him, we see God saying, 'This is what you ought to be like.' Jesus is *the* human being, humanity according to the maker's specifications, the great prototype, the perfect person. He is the model of what all of us, whether male or female, were meant to be.

This is one reason why Jesus came: to be our pattern. When we want to know what we are supposed to be we can look at Jesus. Jesus is *the* standard – the final benchmark against which we examine our lives, the one we ought to imitate. In fact, this makes sound psychological sense; we all know that we learn best by following models.

Now it is very important to realise that Jesus did not *just* come to be our pattern. That would make him no more than a great teacher. The New Testament goes much further and repeatedly interprets Jesus' death as an awesome sacrificial event in which God himself paid the price for the sins of human beings. This is something that we will look at further in the second section.

These, then, are the three standards: the inbuilt moral code, the Ten Rules and, finally, the one perfect life. In moving through these standards it is as if the focus gradually sharpens until finally we see what God wants of us, not in vague or abstract terms, but in a single real life lived out as it ought to be. This, the signposts say, is the right way.

With this in mind, let's move to look at the second part of the great response that God wants – right attitudes.

HAVING RIGHT **ATTITUDES**

What does God want of us? . . . To act justly and to love kindness and to walk humbly with your God.

We have seen what it means for us to 'act justly'. To act justly is critical to finding the right way. To neglect justice is to choose to go in the wrong direction – it is to lose your way entirely. But Micah's message doesn't stop at commanding right actions. God, he says, doesn't just want right actions, he also requires that we 'love kindness'. We need to try to unpack exactly what this means.

Yet before we do that, we need to realise that to 'love kindness' is primarily to do with our attitudes, rather than our actions. In other words, the challenge of walking the right way goes deeper than deeds and words. If actions are to do with the 'exterior' of our lives, to love kindness is to do with the 'interior' of our lives. It focuses on what we are deep down inside. Here, though, some might say, 'If my actions are OK then does it really matter what my attitude is like? Isn't it enough for me just to do the right thing, even if my attitude is a million miles from desiring it?'

The first thing to say here is that quite simply we *cannot* – and *should not* – separate attitudes from actions. What we are as human beings includes our emotions and desires. To concentrate solely on our actions as a measure of what we are is to have a distorted view of things. In fact, the Bible teaches that God sees our heart and judges our thoughts. He is interested in who we are as a whole, not simply in the sort of appearance we present. Although perhaps unpalatable, there is justice to this view of who we are. For instance, many of us claim innocence because we have never committed such things as adultery, murder or fraud. But that may simply be because we have never had either the opportunity or the inclination to commit such acts. The second thing to say is this: what we *think* determines what we *become*. Over time, attitudes can become actions. Not even the greatest hypocrites can totally separate their thoughts from their deeds. If you repeatedly think greedy thoughts, sooner or later you will start doing greedy actions. If you keep thinking angry thoughts, then – sooner or later – you will explode in angry words or deeds. Conversely, if you work at thinking kind thoughts, then kind actions are more likely to follow. The point comes over in Micah where we read:

> What sorrow awaits you who lie awake at night, thinking up evil plans. You rise at dawn and hurry to carry them out, simply because you have the power to do so. When you want a piece of land, you find a way to seize it. When you want someone's house, you take it by fraud and

violence. You cheat a man of his property, stealing his family's inheritance. (Micah 2:1–2)

Here there is no separation between evil thoughts and evil actions.

In fact, it is widely acknowledged that attitudes are important in controlling how we live and whether we are successful or not. But attitudes do not simply alter our chances of success or failure, they direct whether or not we travel along the right way. If our actions are like the front wheels on a car then our attitudes are the steering wheel. And, like turning a steering wheel, small, almost invisible movements can have a major effect on which way we go.

Why is there so much wrong with the human race? And (more pressingly) why is there so much wrong with *my* life? The answer is that at the centre of what we are as people, our attitudes are wrong. But what sort of attitudes are we to have? The answer that Micah gives is that we must 'love kindness'. Underlying the word translated here as 'kindness' is a Hebrew word with a rich and deep meaning. Its very richness has given problems to translators, so that in different Bible versions you may see it as 'mercy', 'loving-kindness', 'unfailing love', 'constant love' or 'steadfast love'. Which one is right? All of them. The kindness we are told to love here has at least three dimensions – it involves love, mercy and faithfulness. Let's consider each dimension in turn.

KINDNESS INVOLVES **LOVE**

The first dimension of the word we have translated as 'kindness' is, quite simply, love. In English, 'love' can be used with a range of meanings which cover everything from having sexual desire to strongly liking some food. And 'love' may be both a choice and an emotion, so that 'loving' and 'being in love' can describe two very different things. Here, though, in this first dimension of kindness, the love that is commanded is primarily the love that is a deliberate choice: it is the love that is the product of the head as much as the heart. To love in this sense is to have the attitude of mind that warmly wishes the very best for someone and wants to show them kindness even though they neither deserve it nor will return it. Think of the following examples:

- A woman who cares for her son, despite the fact that he verbally abuses her constantly.

- A man who looks after a wife who is so ill that she is unrecognisable as the woman he married.

- A woman who shows her concern for an awkward and irritable neighbour by doing her shopping.

Some people show love through actions that they would never consider as love. Think of three more examples:

- An office worker who volunteers to take redundancy so that a needy colleague can stay employed.

- A teacher who spends a lunch break helping a pupil with a topic that they don't understand.

- Someone who spends every Friday night on a soup run working with 'rough sleepers'.

All of these actions fit within the range of the word 'love'. Notice, first, that love is sacrificial. In none of these cases is there the psychological thrill that we often associate with 'romantic' love. Second, while the love shown is an attitude, it is far more than just an attitude. It is an attitude that produces actions. This love is not just something that is commanded by God; it is something demonstrated by him. Love, mercy and faithfulness are described as part of the character of God from the very start of the Bible and, in the New Testament, John summed up the relationship of God to love in the briefest but most dramatic statement possible: 'God is love' (1 John 4:8). And God, at least, practises what he preaches, for as John 3:16 (NIV) tells us: 'God so loved the world that he gave his one and only Son, that whoever believes in him shall not perish but have eternal life.'

It is not surprising, then, that as the ultimate signpost to the right way, Jesus shows love. His actions towards those in need, the sick and the bereaved, mark him out as man of remarkable love. The depth of Jesus' love is revealed in something he said to his followers on the night before he was crucified: 'My command is this: love each other as I have loved you. Greater love has no one than this: to lay down one's life for one's friends' (John 15:12–13, NIV). Jesus sets no limit to love.

When Jesus was asked what the most important commandment was, he answered that it was to 'love the LORD your God with all your heart, all your soul, all your mind, and all your strength,' and to 'love your neighbour as yourself' (Mark 12:30–31). In saying that, Jesus summarised the teaching of the Old Testament. But he redefined even that. So we read in John 13:34 (NIV) that Jesus said to his followers, 'A new command I give you: love one another. As I have loved you, so you must love one another.' Jesus set himself up as the standard of love and commanded that his disciples imitate him in showing love to each other in a similar manner.

While our world longs for the loving side of kindness, it often knows very little of it. We live in a world where 'road rage', 'office rage', 'air rage', 'computer rage' and even 'life rage' is common. You can see it in our humour, where the prevailing mood seems increasingly to be one of savage sarcasm, bitterness and cruelty. Kindness, and particularly this loving type of kindness, is such an unspectacular and overlooked virtue that it is easy to wonder how many of us have ever really desired it.

KINDNESS INVOLVES **MERCY**

The second dimension of kindness is to have mercy. To have mercy is to express love and compassion to others, particularly those who are in need. When we talk about 'being merciful' or 'showing mercy' the images that come to mind are acts of compassion to people who are sick or in prison. And as with other virtues, the meaning of the word 'mercy' is highlighted by thinking of its opposites. To be merciless is to have no forgiveness or pity – it is to pursue someone to the very limit, to take everything they have and to kick them when they are down.

Mercy is more than just another form of kindness – it is something stronger and has two distinguishing characteristics. First, mercy is a response to suffering. So, for example, for someone to give a wealthy person a meal might be an act of kindness, but for them to give a meal to someone who was starving would be an act of mercy. Second, in general, mercy is to show compassion to someone who does not deserve it. So someone pleading guilty in a court and asking for a lenient sentence, or someone who had accumulated bills asking for their debts to be cancelled would be pleas for mercy.

Those who ask for mercy know that they have no right to it; those who are asked to grant mercy know that they cannot be forced to give it. No one has any right to mercy – if they did, it would not be mercy.

Incidentally, mercy is not blind sentiment. To show mercy may indicate that you are soft-hearted but it does not automatically show that you are soft-headed. The best sort of mercy is a wise mercy. So, when faced with a drunk who is begging, to simply give them some cash is not the best sort of mercy, which would be to help them in a better and more lasting way. And, as all doctors (and most parents) know, there are times when, in order to show mercy, it may be necessary to act firmly.

Throughout the Bible, God is the one who is merciful. So in one of Daniel's prayers we read the following: 'We do not make requests of you because we are righteous, but because of your great mercy' (Daniel 9:18, NIV). This emphasises again one of the key aspects of mercy – those who need mercy cannot bargain for it. They can only plead. After King David had sinned, he began his prayer of repentance like this, 'Have mercy on me, O God, because of your unfailing love. Because of your great compassion, blot out the stain of my sins' (Psalm 51:1). Both Daniel and David expected mercy because of who God is. They didn't demand it and they didn't try to pretend that they had earned it; they knew that mercy is always a free gift.

Because God is merciful, he has commanded his people to be merciful as well. Indeed, part of God's complaint against his people in Micah's day was that, because of all their injustice, they had ceased to be merciful.

In the New Testament, the ideas of mercy focus around Jesus in three ways. First, Jesus taught that we could only be rescued by God's mercy. In one of the stories Jesus told, a religious leader and a dishonest tax collector went to the temple to pray. The religious leader prayed with confidence, drawing God's attention to his own virtues. In contrast, the other man did things differently: he 'stood at a distance and dared not even lift his eyes to heaven as he prayed. Instead, he beat his chest in sorrow, saying, "O God, be merciful to me, for I am a sinner"' (Luke 18:13). Jesus concluded his story by saying that it was this 'sinner', not the religious leader, who returned home right with God.

Second, Jesus modelled what it is to show mercy. So when a blind man shouted out repeatedly – 'Jesus, have mercy on me!' Jesus answered his request by healing him. Similarly, he showed mercy to lepers, those struggling under the influence of evil, the hungry and the bereaved. He said to his followers, 'Be merciful, just as your Father is merciful' (Luke 6:36, NIV).

Third, the writers of the New Testament see God's mercy as being focused in Jesus Christ. It is as if Jesus has become the channel through which God pours out mercy to a needy world. So we read: 'Therefore, it was necessary for him to be made in every respect like us, his brothers and sisters, so that he could be our merciful and faithful High Priest before God' (Hebrews 2:17). Whereas an Old Testament Jew would have gone to the temple to seek God's mercy, Jesus' followers see him personally as the place where mercy is to be found.

If our world badly needs love, it also needs mercy. Looking around us, we will certainly find those who desperately need mercy. In our families there may be those who are in trouble and who need us to show them mercy. In our workplaces there will be those for whom life is miserable and to whom we can show mercy. And in our communities there are almost certainly those who are lonely, mentally disturbed, debt-ridden or in trouble. And you only have to read the newspapers or watch the television to see the need for mercy among the nations of the world: there are many millions who are hungry, oppressed or abused.

It is all too easy today to adopt the mood of our culture, shrug our shoulders and say, 'But it's none of my business.' To have the mercy dimension of kindness in our lives is to say that it *is* our business and we will do what we can to help.

If the call to be merciful seems hard, it is worth remembering Jesus' words: 'Blessed are the merciful, for they will be shown mercy' (Matthew 5:7, NIV). To fail to show mercy to others suggests that we have not understood that God wants to be merciful to us.

KINDNESS INVOLVES
FAITHFULNESS

The third dimension of the kindness that God wants is faithfulness. Faithfulness is about loyalty and commitment and – above all – the keeping of promises. In a world that thrives on emotions, faithfulness is an overlooked virtue. Today, the main motive for doing anything is because you 'feel like it' and, if you don't feel like it, you don't do it. The results of this thinking are seen everywhere: in marriage, in society and in business practice. We have shifted from a culture where people kept agreements because their values demanded that they did, to one where agreements are kept because otherwise the lawyers will get you. Without faithfulness, love and mercy would just be flashes of emotion. Faithfulness puts the staying power in kindness; it kindles sparks into flames of effective action.

As with the other dimensions of kindness, God is a model for faithfulness. The idea of faithfulness is linked – in the strongest way – with the idea of the covenant, the great theme of the Bible. The key point about a covenant is that it is a binding contract between two parties that both sides promise to keep. The Old Testament tells how God, out of love, declared a covenant with his people and promised to love and deliver them and how, in response, his people promised to obey God and worship him. The Old Testament goes on to tell how, despite the fact that God's people failed over the centuries to keep the conditions of the covenant, God remained faithful and kept his promises. The New Testament tells how, through Jesus, God made a new covenant – one that was no longer limited to the people of Israel but extends to all those from whatever background who come to God through Christ.

That God is the one who is faithful and who can always be trusted is a truth found throughout the Bible. Deuteronomy 7:9 (NIV) sums up God's character: 'Know therefore that the LORD your God is God; he is the faithful God, keeping his covenant of love to a thousand generations of those who love him and keep his commandments.' In Micah's prophetic warnings to his people, perhaps the ultimate issue is that the people have failed to be faithful to the covenant. God has kept his side of the covenant; it is time for his people to keep theirs.

In the New Testament, Jesus is the model for faithfulness. He is obedient to God even to the point of dying on the cross. The devil tempts him to be unfaithful but he resists. Jesus is the 'merciful and faithful High Priest before God' (Hebrews 2:17) and in the great visions of Revelation Jesus is described as being the 'faithful witness'. Millions of Christians have found Jesus to be faithful.

As God – Father and Son and Spirit – is faithful, so we need to be faithful. We need to be people who treat promises seriously and whose word can be trusted. This call to faithfulness occurs in all sorts of areas. Clearly, one major area where faithfulness is often neglected today is in marriage. Indeed, it is in the context of marriage that the word 'faithful' is most widely used today. Yet, the idea of being faithful has a far wider reference than marriage. It is vital in any sort of friendship – no deep relationship of trust can be built between two people unless there is some sort of loyalty or faithfulness between them. Faithfulness is also an important element in making any sort of commitment in any area of life. It is all too easy to undertake some grand and worthwhile project and to give it up after the first few discouragements. But to be faithful is to say, 'I promised I would do this, so I will indeed do it.' It is to keep going. There is a story of a man touring Calcutta with Mother Teresa and visiting a house where terminally ill children were cared for. As he watched Mother Teresa at work, the man was overwhelmed by the sheer scale of the suffering all around her. 'How can you bear the load without being crushed by it?' he asked. Mother Teresa's reply was simple, 'I am not called to be successful; I am called to be faithful.'

To be faithful is also to be reliable. We all know people – some of us are fortunate to be married to them – who can be relied upon. They are like rocks and, whatever happens, they are always there to give counsel and support. Kindness of any sort, whether it is full of love or mercy, means very little unless it is maintained. Whether in our families, our work or our community, we need to be people who are known to be faithful.

To love kindness involves desiring three things: love, mercy and faithfulness. It is to long to be someone who cares for other people, who wants their best and who is committed to them. It is to desire to live in a way that is totally contrary to the standards of our world, where putting self-interest and personal pleasure first is the norm.

Kindness has other virtues. For instance, it is remarkable how it is capable of bringing good out of bad situations. Talk to anyone who has been involved in some accident or tragedy and they will often point to how some act of kindness shed a great light in the darkness. Kindness also breeds kindness and has the ability to disarm anger and irritation. As the saying goes, kindness is the oil that takes the friction out of life. Kindness is also surprisingly memorable; we remember kind people – and remember them with more affection – long after our memories of the eloquent or the witty have faded.

HOW CAN WE WALK
THE RIGHT WAY?

Through this section, we have looked at walking the right way in life. We have seen that to walk the right way is both to act justly and to love kindness: to have a life of both right actions and right attitudes. We have also seen the three great standards of the right way to live – the inbuilt moral code, the Ten Rules and the one perfect life of Jesus. We have been shown the way.

But we need more than this. If we have taken seriously what has been said so far, then our reaction must be that the way is too hard for us. Quite simply, the universal experience of every human being other than Jesus is that walking the right way of life is too demanding. Who can truly say that they act justly? Who can, in all honesty, admit that they fully love kindness with its three dimensions of love, mercy and faithfulness? And the three standards, even if we treat them simply as pointers to the right way, only make matters worse. As we saw, even if we just take the inbuilt universal moral code we still find that we fail this most general of standards. The Ten Commandments are still more severe, and against the standard of the one perfect life of Jesus, even the best people admit that they fail.

So, have we reached a dead end? Has God simply set out the way and defined the standards for how it should be walked so that we all fail hopelessly? Thankfully, no! There is good news, the very best of news. The rest of this book is about how God has come to the road himself so that we can walk along the way of life with him. In doing this he supplies the three things we need. Firstly, he himself offers us rescue: he has provided a means by which those of us who have lost – or left – the way can get back on to it. Second, he has personally provided us with a guide for the way – Jesus. Third, he has himself provided the power for us to walk the way – the Holy Spirit. Without God, the way is impossible but if we choose to walk *with* God, we are offered rescue, help and strength.

The next part of this book explores how we can begin to learn to walk with God.

LEARNING TO WALK WITH GOD

So far, we have considered how we walk the way of life. However, we find ourselves in a predicament. We can recognise the three great standards that act as signposts to the way, but it seems that this is not enough. The problem is not *knowing* what is right, it is *doing* what is right. The demands posed by walking the way of life are too great. If we are honest, however hard we try, even the best of us find ourselves either drifting off the way or going in the wrong direction entirely. We need help, but only God's help will do. The possibility that Micah mentions – that we can walk with God – comes as good news. But who is the God we should seek to walk the way of life with? And how do we approach him? These are questions that we need to answer.

11

FIVE PORTRAITS OF **GOD**

It is impossible to give an adequate picture of God – even to begin to summarise what the Bible tells us about God would take an entire book. Yet, here, the theme of this book helps us – this is, after all, a practical guide to walking the way of life and so the next few chapters cover those aspects of God that are particularly relevant to those who want to walk the right way of life with him.

When we think of people, there are two ways we can describe them. One way would be to describe them by their characteristics: for example, their age, weight, height and educational background. Another way would be to describe them in terms of how they relate to other people: perhaps as a parent, friend or manager. In practice, this second way is actually more valuable. It is far more common to hear people praised for how they have related to others than for what they are. When someone asks, 'What's your boss like?' they are probably not expecting a physical description for an answer; they are expecting details of what they are like to work for. The same principle applies to God; it is how God relates to us as people that we find most helpful.

This viewpoint is actually the emphasis of the Bible. Although the Bible does teach facts about God (for example, that he is glorious, eternal and all-knowing), those facts are revealed in passing. The Bible is less about teaching us and more about gaining a response from us: God reveals who he is in order that we should turn to him and become his followers.

This raises an important point that needs to be understood. It centres on the fact that there are two totally different views about how people walk with God. The view held by most religions is something like this. To walk with God is extraordinarily difficult: if you manage to achieve the right level of spiritual discipline and a suitably advanced level of insight, then God may (and only may) allow you to have access to him and – if you are especially good – to accompany him. The picture you get is that walking with God is like keeping pace with some Olympic-class athlete going flat out; it is almost impossible. In contrast, the view of the Bible is very different. Here, God is someone who desires that people walk with him and makes every effort for them to do so. It is as if God slows his pace and extends a helping hand in order that anybody can, if they will, walk with him. The Bible teaches the great concept of grace – the idea that God bends down towards us and offers to help us. Our task is not the impossible one of earning God's favour; it is the possible one of accepting it.

In order for our relationship with God to begin and develop, there are things that must be done in our lives. There are five things in particular that God desires to do: he wants to rescue, forgive, adopt, guide and transform us. It may be helpful to think of these five actions that God wants to undertake in our lives as being like five portraits, each of which shows one particular aspect of who God is. In order to become someone who walks with God, it is vital to understand at least something of each of these aspects of who God is. And to stay walking with God there is nothing better than to go and gaze at these portraits again and learn more of God's nature.

Before we look at these five actions, it is important to realise why God wants to rescue, forgive, adopt, guide and transform us. What motivates him? The extraordinary answer the Bible gives is that God does these things for us out of love. God loves men and women so much that he has gone to the extraordinary lengths of coming as Jesus Christ to die for us. God's love is even more remarkable because it is not, as much human love is, based on wishful thinking. He is under no illusions about what we are like. In spite of what God knows about us – and that is more than we know about ourselves – he loves us, and this love is the motive for his actions towards us. God, as Saint Augustine said sixteen centuries ago, 'loves each one of us as if there was only the one of us'.

A final point here is that in this part of the book there are more Bible references than there have been so far. This is unavoidable because the Bible is our source of reliable knowledge about God. We cannot analyse God or describe him from our own senses; our minds are incapable of examining who God is. As John Wesley remarked in the eighteenth century, 'Bring me a worm that can comprehend man and I will show you a man who can comprehend God.' Our own speculations on who God is, and what he might be like, have little value compared to God's own statements about himself. If God had not spoken, we would have to be silent.

12

THE GOD WHO **RESCUES US**

In considering the image of 'the way' that we have used in the first part of this book, we realised that we are lost. We have ignored the signposts, taken wrong turnings and, all too often, chosen to leave the way altogether. To get lost on the way of life is actually a very serious matter.

First, we are *hopelessly* lost. The Bible repeatedly uses the image of lost sheep to describe the plight of human beings. So, in Isaiah 53:6, the universal predicament of the human race is summed up like this: 'All of us, like sheep, have strayed away. We have left God's paths to follow our own.' In the dry and wild lands of the Middle East, sheep need many things in order to survive – water, grass and protection from dangerous animals – and the task of a shepherd is to provide all of these. A sheep that wanders away from the flock and its shepherd is vulnerable and in serious trouble. To be a lost sheep is not to be like someone who, having made a poor choice of the route home, is merely going to be slightly late for supper – it is to be like someone lost in a wilderness who, unless they are rescued, is never going to get home at all.

Second, human beings are *helplessly* lost. We live in an age of self-help and positive thinking, where it is common to imagine that all we need to solve any problem is determination, initiative and self-confidence. Yet the biblical picture of the human situation is darker but more realistic – we cannot fix the problem of the human race ourselves; we *are* the problem. Our danger is such that it is beyond the scope of self-help; we need a rescuer.

Rescue is one of the great themes of the Bible. Its pages are full of people who are rescued from floods, slavery, thirst, defeat and other dangers. And it is not just individuals who are rescued; it is whole nations as well. In the Old Testament we read how God's people literally lost the way twice, ending up in the wrong country, first as slaves in Egypt and second as captives in Babylon. Yet in both cases, God rescued them.

The great plot-line of the Bible, from the first page of Genesis to the last page of Revelation, could be summarised as 'the rescue of the human race'. In Genesis 3 we read how Adam and Eve disobeyed God, rebelled against him and, as a result, lost the privileged relationship with God that they had had. Ever since, the human race has followed their example. The Bible is plain; something is badly wrong with the human race. We need rescuing.

In fact, many words in the Bible such as 'redemption', 'deliverance' and 'salvation' are really terms for different types of rescue. Another idea linked to the concept of rescue is that of the Messiah. Jews at the end of Old Testament times looked forward to the coming of the Messiah, the king who would rescue them from all their enemies. Jesus' followers claimed that he was the Messiah and used the equivalent Greek word, *Christos*, of him. So today, whenever we talk of Jesus Christ, we are really remembering him as 'Jesus the rescuer'.

If sheep are, because of their vulnerability and foolishness, an accurate (if unflattering) image of how human beings get lost, so shepherds tend to be an image of their rescuers. For instance, in Ezekiel 34:1–9, God describes how his people have become like lost sheep and announces judgement on their leaders as failing shepherds. Then, remarkably, in verses 10–16, he says this:

> I will rescue my flock from their mouths . . . I myself will search and find my sheep. I will be like a shepherd looking for his scattered flock. I will find my sheep and rescue them from all the places where they were scattered . . . I myself will tend my sheep and give them a place to lie down in peace . . . I will search for my lost ones who strayed away, and I will bring them safely home again. I will bandage the injured and strengthen the weak.

The repetition of the word 'I' here is striking: God is promising that he, *personally*, will bring back the lost sheep.

In the New Testament, Jesus picks up this prophecy and applies it to himself. So, in John 10:11 (NIV), we read this: 'I am the good shepherd. The good shepherd lays down his life for the sheep.' Two things are notable here. First, the Bible makes it plain that God personally goes and rescues human beings. He doesn't entrust our rescue to angels or some other intermediaries; instead, he does it himself. Second, Jesus hints that the rescue of the lost sheep will be achieved at the cost of his own death.

In the letters of the New Testament, the idea that, in Jesus, God was rescuing his people is widely repeated. In Galatians 1:4 we find Paul writing this, 'Jesus gave his life for our sins, just as God our Father planned, in order to rescue us from this evil world in which we live.' We see, then, that in order to rescue us, God became one of us. But what is it that Jesus has rescued us *from*? There are at least four overlapping areas where God offers rescue.

First, God offers *rescue from the past*. All too often we find that people are trapped by what has happened in their lives. We hear such sad comments as, 'I failed there,' 'I messed up on that' or – most tragically of all, 'If only I had done something different.' Like some great spider's web, the threads of the past tend to bind us into lives of regret, failure and futility. Jesus can set us free from such things.

Second, God offers *rescue from fear.* Fear, whether of failure, the future or death, haunts many people. If you do not know God, life is an unpredictable rollercoaster ride through a lonely and uncaring world that abruptly ends with the dark and fearsome silence of death. If you do know God, however, all that changes. Life is no longer a journey into darkness but one into light; it is no longer a lonely journey but one with God as a companion.

Third, God offers *rescue from evil.* In several places in the New Testament, Jesus is seen as the one who rescues God's people from the influence and control of evil supernatural powers. The Bible makes it clear that such forces exist, that they enslave people and that only Christ can offer rescue from them. For some people, becoming a follower of Jesus is accompanied by a dramatic experience of liberation from the control of evil. Of course, evil does not go away completely when someone becomes a follower of Jesus. Although evil may have lost its dominating power, it remains a troubling influence that will have to be fought until death. This is something that we will return to in the final part of this book.

God also offers *rescue from guilt.* The issues of guilt and forgiveness are so important that they are treated on their own in the next chapter.

Three final points need mentioning briefly. First, the Christian's rescue is, so far, only a partial one. The first stage of the rescue is complete – a great victory has been won and we have been liberated from the control of evil.

Nevertheless, the legacy of evil persists and, although they have lost much of their former power over us, things like sickness, death and sin remain. Yet one day our rescue will be completed and these things will be no more. Think of a man who is imprisoned in some dreadful jail. One day, the door of his cell is opened and in walks his lawyer with his release papers. The prisoner shouts out in his excitement, 'I am free! I have been rescued!' Is he correct to get so excited? Of course. He is indeed free, despite the fact that he has yet to leave his cell and walk through the gloomy prison before the doors to the outside world are flung open before him. Christians are in a similar position – declared free but not yet quite out of captivity.

Second, while the Christian's rescue may so far be only partial, there can be no doubt that it will finally be achieved. The basis of this certainty is the resurrection of Jesus Christ. Prior to that event, death and evil had reigned unchallenged over the human race. Everybody, without exception, died and stayed dead. Now, with Jesus, the process has been reversed and for the first time death and evil have been defeated, their iron grip on the human race broken. Death is like some grim, locked chamber into which people vanish, never to return. Jesus' resurrection is not only the first exception to the rule, it marks the breaking of the lock on the chamber door.

Third, and finally, while this portrait of God as rescuer is primarily one of God himself, it is also a picture of what we should be like. The principle that God's people are to be rescuers, because they have been rescued, has given the motive for centuries of Christian work with those who are sick, poor and suffering. So, for instance, in the Britain of the early nineteenth century it was keen followers of Jesus such as William Wilberforce, Lord Shaftesbury, Hannah Moore and Josephine Butler who led campaigns for the abolition of slavery, the reform of prisons, the ending of child prostitution, legislation on factory conditions and the founding of orphanages. In our own time, Charles Colson – a man who, before his conversion to Christ, was considered by the media to be a politician 'incapable of humanitarian thought' – has worked to reform the US prison service and set up a movement of more than 50,000 voluntary prison workers operating in 88 countries.

God is the great rescuer and his people are to follow his lead.

13

THE GOD WHO **FORGIVES US**

In looking at the portrait of God as our rescuer, we were reminded how human beings have left the right way and are badly lost. This is a serious predicament but according to the Bible the reality is actually much worse. It is not as though, through no fault of our own, we have become accidentally lost; it is that we have become lost because of our own wrong actions. In legal terms human beings are not 'innocent victims'; we are instead, 'guilty parties'. Our desperate situation arises not from our ignorance but from our own wilful choice. We are on the wrong way because we have rebelled from God, have purposely ignored the signposts and have deliberately followed the wrong way. As a result, we are guilty and need to seek God's forgiveness.

Such a view is unpopular today. Many people feel uncomfortable about Christianity's analysis of the ultimate problem of the human race as centring on personal guilt and sin. Our culture emphasises having a 'positive assessment of yourself'; it has little place for the ideas of sin and repentance. In considering this issue, five points are worth noting.

First, the fact that we do not like what an analysis says shouldn't blind us to the really important point of an analysis – is it true? It would be foolish to walk out of a doctor's surgery and tear up the prescription we had been given, simply because we didn't like the diagnosis!

Second, to object that it is the Bible – and Christianity – that makes us guilty, is a classic case of 'shooting the messenger'. We are already guilty because of what we ourselves have done. The Bible is like a bright light shining into a dirty room; it has simply revealed what was already there.

Third, if Christianity delivered a verdict of 'guilty' on human beings and nothing more, then we could argue that it was cruel. But the message of the Bible is a message of guilt *and* forgiveness, of disease *and* cure. The message of Jesus is called the 'gospel', a word that, quite simply, means 'good news'.

Fourth, the negative imagery of being a 'forgiven sinner' is balanced in a truly biblical Christianity by the wonderful truth that we are adopted as God's children and can come to know God as a perfect heavenly Father.

Fifth, the reality is that, however they are described (or disguised), issues of guilt and sin occur in all our lives. Guilt is rife in our society today. As psychologist Erich Fromm has written, 'It is indeed amazing that in as fundamentally irreligious a culture as ours, the sense of guilt should be so widespread and deeply rooted as it is.' In some cases, issues of guilt may manifest themselves simply as a quiet but unhappy feeling that our lives have fallen short of our own standards. In other cases, there may be a sharp and painful recognition that in some specific case we have done something very bad or wrong. Only knowing forgiveness will cure such issues. Ignoring them, or rationalising them away, will merely suppress them.

With those comments in mind, let's move on to look at forgiveness. Here, we return to the 'mercy' dimension of kindness. If we were to imagine how God might best show us mercy, we might be inclined to think first of how he could improve our finances, our health or our state of mind. The truth is that, of all the needs we have, our deepest need is for forgiveness. It is not simply that without forgiveness we remain guilty; it is that without forgiveness our relationship with God is broken. Unless we know forgiveness there remains a break in our relationship with God that will prevent us walking with him.

How can the relationship be restored? There are three basic steps to restore any relationship, whether human or divine.

First, the one who has committed the offence must repent. To repent involves making a U-turn; it combines a recognition that you have been going on the wrong road with a decision to get back onto the right road. In repentance, there must be both an acknowledgement of wrongdoing and a determination to do right.

Second, the wrong action that caused the problem must be resolved. Actions have consequences and there is often a price to pay. If it is at all possible, what has been done wrong must be put right. In some cases, a penalty or punishment must be borne.

Third, there must be an offer of forgiveness by the one who has been offended. To forgive someone is deliberately to decide to overlook what has happened to you. To use a financial image, it is to cancel a debt. Forgetting and forgiving are often confused yet they are different. *Forgiving* is a decision that can be made in a moment: you can tear up a bill in a second. Forgetting – 'refusing to remember' is a better expression – is, in contrast, a long-term process that may involve many repeated decisions. To forget in this sense is to choose to force the memory of some offence out of your mind whenever it surfaces. If you think of the offence as being like a wound, then to forgive is to allow the wound to be sewn up; to forget is to allow it to heal. A failure to choose to forget can undo the good work of the initial forgiving; it is just as if the wound becomes septic. Thankfully, God forgives *and* forgets.

In the Bible, we see that God invites repentance and offers forgiveness. We see too, how, in a staggering act of grace, he personally offers to resolve the wrongs by paying the penalty himself. Using a range of images, the New Testament talks about Christ 'atoning for us', 'ransoming us' or 'paying the price' for our wrongdoings in order that we may be forgiven. Jesus himself summed up his mission like this: 'For even the Son of Man came not to be served but to serve others and to give his life as a ransom for many' (Mark 10:45). The idea that Jesus was making peace between humanity and God through his death is a theme that runs throughout the New Testament. In 1 Corinthians 15:3 Paul sums up the entire matter in the fewest words possible, 'I passed on to you what was most important and what had also been passed on to me. Christ died for our sins.'

In thinking about God as our rescuer we saw hints that his rescue action would be sacrificial – the good shepherd was going to lay down his life for the sheep. Here, what was only hinted at is made plain. In order to offer us forgiveness, Christ – God's Son, God in human form – must die. Plainly, God goes far more than halfway to meet us in order to restore the relationship and he pays a heavy price for our forgiveness. Forgiveness is not just our greatest need, it is also God's highest achievement.

History has shown that it is all too easy to take God's forgiveness for granted or see it as some general principle automatically applied to everybody whether they like it or not. Yet it must be something that each one of us takes to heart personally. The apostle Paul did this; he wrote, 'I live in this earthly body by trusting in the Son of God, who loved me and gave himself for me' (Galatians 2:20). Paul's awareness that, through Christ's death, God had lovingly forgiven him was something that transformed him totally.

Micah's statement, which runs through this book, ended with the command for the people to 'walk humbly with their God'. To recognise that we have to be forgiven – and at an awesome cost – is helpful in encouraging humility; not even the greatest saint can ever walk proudly with God. We walk with God only because he has gone to almost unimaginable lengths to allow us to do so.

Finally, we saw at the end of the last chapter that God's rescue of us is meant to be a model for our actions to others: having been rescued ourselves we are ready to rescue others. The portrait of God is to be a pattern for us to emulate. This pattern of imitation is repeated even more strongly with forgiveness; we are to be forgivers too. That our forgiveness is linked with our forgiveness of others is made clear by Jesus in the Lord's Prayer: 'and forgive us our sins, as we have forgiven those who sin against us' (Matthew 6:12). Paul says much the same thing. 'Make allowance for each other's faults, and forgive anyone who offends you. Remember, the Lord forgave you, so you must forgive others' (Colossians 3:13). We are to be those who are both forgiven and forgiving.

14

THE GOD WHO **ADOPTS US**

In the last two chapters we have seen how, in Jesus Christ, God *rescues* us so that we can go from being lost to being found, and *forgives* us so that we can go from being one of his enemies to being one of his friends. But it gets even better. In the Bible we also learn that God's great purpose does not end at creating people who are rescued friends but that he seeks to make people who now know him as their perfect 'heavenly Father'. To do this, God adopts those who come to him through Jesus and, in effect, says to them, 'I know what you were. But I now make you my child and grant you all the rights and privileges that go with that position.'

Despite being central to Christian teaching, the idea that God desires to adopt men and women so that they can know him as 'Father' is often neglected. In the Old Testament, God is described as having some of the characteristics of a good parent but there is no suggestion that he could be addressed as 'Father'. Jesus, however, was very conscious of being God's Son and, when praying, always addressed God as 'Father'. Even more remarkably, Jesus taught that his followers could know

God in a similar way – the prayer he taught them began 'Our Father in heaven'. The apostle John says that 'to all who believed him [Jesus] and accepted him, he gave the right to become children of God' (John 1:12). Paul explains and expands this:

> God sent him [Jesus] to buy freedom for us who were slaves to the law, so that he could adopt us as his very own children. And because we are his children, God has sent the Spirit of his Son into our hearts, prompting us to call out, 'Abba, Father.' Now you are no longer a slave but God's own child. And since you are his child, God has made you his heir. (Galatians 4:5–7)

The idea that we can know God as our heavenly Father is one of the greatest truths of Christianity but can also be one of the hardest to embrace. However, Jesus never let human fatherhood define how God is a Father. Instead, he described the qualities of God that make him Father. We find out that God is loving, fair, caring, patient and prepared to suffer for the wellbeing of his children. Quite simply, God the Father is like Jesus and Jesus himself said, 'Anyone who has seen me has seen the Father!' (John 14:9). The emphasis of the Bible in calling God 'Father' is on him being the perfect parent.

But what, exactly, does it mean to be adopted by God? When we think of adoption today we think of a child being put into a new family in order that they might have emotional, psychological and physical security. It is an important process. Yet in Bible times adoption was even more important because the family was the source of education, social status, employment and financial security. To move from one family system to another was to have every aspect of your life transformed totally. Becoming a child of God is equally radical and there are several major implications. Let's consider three of them.

First, we have *the privilege of access to the Father.* We can now come to God with confidence. Most of us have grown up in a Christian or post-Christian culture and take for granted the idea that we can treat God as our personal heavenly Father. Yet in non-Christian religions to hold such a belief is either presumption or a heresy. Outside the Christian faith, the best you can hope for is that God will accept you as a faithful servant or a good slave, a relationship that is very much inferior. So, for instance, slaves or servants have only limited access to their master, they may have to go through an intermediary, they may have to wait and there will be a limit on what and how much they can say. Above all, hanging over every aspect of the relationship, is some degree of fear or unease. However, as children of God, we can have a confidence that God hears our prayers. As Paul notes this in his letter to the Romans:

> So you have not received a spirit that makes you fearful slaves. Instead, you received God's Spirit when he adopted you as his own children. Now we call him,

'Abba, Father.' For his Spirit joins with our spirit to affirm that we are God's children. And since we are his children, we are his heirs. In fact, together with Christ we are heirs of God's glory. (Romans 8:15–17)

Second, being adopted also gives us *the privilege of assurance of our future.* Think again about a slave or a servant – not only do they have no right to talk to their master, they have no certainty about their status. A slave or servant who is favoured today can be thrown out of the household tomorrow. Psychologically, this is very harmful; being a slave or a servant is hardly a relationship in which confidence, trust and assurance flourish. To be a child of God, and to know that, is to be wonderfully set free. It is to be assured that God's attitude to us will not change and that his love will continue.

Third, we have *the privilege of an association with God's family.* When we have God as our Father, we also gain brothers and sisters. We are no longer individuals; we become part of a family. Various things follow from this. For one thing, we gain Jesus as a brother. Jesus taught that his followers were his family (Matthew 12:48–50) and, when resurrected, referred to his disciples as 'his brothers' (Matthew 28:10; John 20:17). So when we become believers in Jesus, not only do we gain him as our brother, we also gain other Christians as brothers and sisters. We are adopted into a vast family. Other followers of Jesus are our brothers and sisters in Christ.

Of course, the glorious truth that we are adopted comes with a great responsibility. As we are now part of God's family we must live up to the family standard and behave appropriately. We must make sure that nothing we do drags the name of Jesus and other Christians down into the dirt. The honour of God's family must be upheld. The idea that we have such a responsibility should remove any temptation to presume on our relationship with God our Father. To take God for granted and to live in a careless and selfish way is to abuse our relationship with God.

The idea that God desires to adopt us is a vital one and one we should not neglect. It moves our relationship with God out of the chill sternness of the courtroom setting in which guilt and forgiveness are discussed, into the affectionate warmth of the family home. Those who find the title 'forgiven sinner' depressing, may need to realise that it is balanced by the title of 'loved child'.

Three final points are relevant. One, when talking about the idea of adoption, the Bible often refers to the Holy Spirit. One of the main roles of the Holy Spirit is to make that personal bond between human beings and God. He is the link person – the intermediary – between God and his children and also between the children and each other.

Two, the Bible sees our adoption as sons and daughters as, so far, incomplete. It is as if we have received the full title of being a child of God but, as yet, only some of the benefits. In Romans 8:23, Paul says: 'And we believers also groan, even though we have the Holy Spirit within us as a foretaste of future glory, for we long for our bodies to be released from sin and suffering. We, too, wait with eager hope for the day when God will give us our full rights as his adopted children, including the new bodies he has promised us.' One day, whether at our death or at Christ's coming again, we will be given new bodies and will finally triumph over all that drags us down. We will have come into our full inheritance.

Three, as with the other portraits of God, this one is also a pattern for us. God adopts people by seeking them out and bringing them into his family. In our own way, we are to try to do the same. Our goals should be to turn enemies into friends and friends into brothers and sisters. The idea of God as 'the one who adopts' has a further significance. In an age where corporate business provides the accepted standard for how any organisation is to work, the concept of adoption reminds us that churches are to have another model. We are to be *family*.

The idea that God allows us to be his adopted children should change how we think about walking with God. Instead of following a leader who has no apparent concern about whether those behind them can keep up, think instead of a parent walking along with a child. They slow their pace to allow the child to keep up, hold hands with them for encouragement and are constantly watching for problems and hazards. On the most difficult patches, they may even bend down and carry the youngster. For those who have come to know God through Jesus, the great truth is that it is this image that most accurately shows how we walk with God.

15

THE GOD WHO **GUIDES US**

So far in this section, we have seen how God rescues, forgives and adopts his people. Faced with walking the way of life, this is enormously encouraging. But if we left matters here, we would be in the position of someone who had been rescued by the emergency services but who was then put back on the way and told, with a farewell wave of the hand, 'OK, you are on your own now.' God, however, does not simply rescue his people and leave them to mess up again. He accompanies them as a guide and protector. This idea is one of the richest seams of the Bible but what does it mean to have a guide? Imagine you were travelling across some difficult and dangerous terrain – perhaps a jungle or some high, rugged mountain landscape – then you might well decide to take a guide. Their role would be to lead, help and protect you and God does the same.

God *leads* us in many ways. Leading is important – it is not enough to be sure you are on the right way, you must also make sure that you are heading in the right direction, and God leads us by giving us his word, the Bible, as a guide to the way. However, he goes further than just giving us advice. In the Old Testament, he himself was literally the guide for his people. When the Israelites left Egypt and began their journey through the wilderness of Sinai, God went in front of them as a pillar of cloud by day and a pillar of fire by night. That is a very dramatic image of how God guides his people. Another image of guidance is found in Psalm 23, where God is portrayed as the shepherd of his people.

> The LORD is my shepherd; I have all that I need.
>
> He lets me rest in green meadows;
>
> he leads me beside peaceful streams.
>
> He renews my strength.
>
> He guides me along right paths,
>
> bringing honour to his name.
>
> (Psalm 23:1–3)

Here, there is a picture of the shepherd going ahead with the sheep following behind, confident in the shepherd's ability to keep them safe. In the New Testament, the letter to the Hebrews ends with a prayer that refers to Jesus as 'the great Shepherd of the sheep, [who] ratified an eternal covenant with his blood' (Hebrews 13:20). This is fitting because, in his life and death, Jesus modelled everything that a shepherd ought to be. He looked after his disciples, kept them safe and claimed that he was the one whom people should follow. For example, in John 8:12 (NIV), we read, '[Jesus] said, "I am the light of the world. Whoever follows me will never walk in darkness, but will have the light of life."' The idea that Jesus is the one who leads his people comes over in the extraordinary claim he makes in John 14:6 – 'I am the way, the truth, and the life. No one can come to the Father except through me.' Here it is as if Jesus is saying 'You are worried about finding the way? Don't worry. Just follow me.'

The Bible makes it clear that one of the main tasks of the Holy Spirit is to continue Jesus' role of *leading* God's people and on the night before the crucifixion Jesus told his disciples that, 'When the Spirit of truth comes, he will guide you into all truth. He will not speak on his own but will tell you what he has heard' (John 16:13). The Holy Spirit guides in two ways: indirectly, by applying God's word to our lives as we read it; and directly, by giving wisdom and insight in specific circumstances. Both are valuable and it is wise to be open to the Spirit's working in either way. As Paul writes, 'Since we are living by the Spirit, let us follow the Spirit's leading in every part of our lives' (Galatians 5:25).

The second aspect of God being our guide is that God *helps* us along the way. This is very encouraging – after all, it would be possible to have a guide who simply stood by and offered helpful advice. God, however, comes alongside us to help us on the way. In thinking about how God helps us we see a similar pattern to how he leads us. In the Old Testament, we read how God strengthens his people. In the New Testament, we see how Jesus helps his disciples and how, on his return to heaven, the Spirit is sent to help all followers of Jesus everywhere. As Jesus made plain to his disciples the night before the crucifixion: 'I will ask the Father, and he will give you another Advocate, who will never leave you. He is the Holy Spirit, who leads into all truth' (John 14:16–17). The word translated 'Advocate' here means 'Comforter', 'Encourager' or 'Counsellor' – someone who is called alongside to help – and could be translated 'Helper'. Jesus is saying to his disciples, 'Whatever I was to you, so the Spirit will be from now on.' As we walk the way of life, so the Holy Spirit comes alongside to strengthen us. Where God guides, he also *helps*.

The third aspect of God being our guide is that he *protects* us. The Bible is under no illusions that the way of life is trouble-free. Indeed, it is quietly insistent that we face not only hazards en route but also enemies. The need for a protector is clearly seen in Psalm 23, where the shepherd is seen as being more than just a guide:

> Even when I walk through the darkest valley,
>
> I will not be afraid, for you are close beside me.
>
> Your rod and your staff protect and comfort me.
>
> (Psalm 23:4)

Throughout the Bible we see men and women in need of God's protection. In many cases, the references are to

God being like some fixed place of protection, 'a refuge', a 'stronghold' and a 'safe shelter'. In other cases, they refer to the protection of God or his angelic forces, as Psalm 91:11 says, 'For he will order his angels to protect you wherever you go.' These promises offer no guarantee of a trouble-free life; walking the way of life remains a challenge even when we walk it with God. Yet while we may not be protected *from* trouble, we are protected *through* trouble.

Those who walk with God will face enemies on the way. In his letter to the followers of Jesus in Ephesus, Paul mentions the forces that confront believers in Jesus. 'Put on all of God's armour so that you will be able to stand firm against all strategies of the devil. For we are not fighting against flesh-and-blood enemies, but against evil rulers and authorities of the unseen world, against mighty powers in this dark world, and against evil spirits in the heavenly places' (Ephesians 6:11–12). It is a daunting list of enemies. Despite this, the New Testament echoes to the sound of victory: Christ has triumphed!

Paul himself expresses the nature of the victory in his letter to the Colossians; here we read God 'cancelled the record of the charges against us and took it away by nailing it to the cross. In this way, he disarmed the spiritual rulers and authorities. He shamed them publicly by his victory over them on the cross' (Colossians 2:14–15). At the end of the Bible, in the book of Revelation, many of the themes of God as guide reappear. So, in Revelation 7:17 we read: 'For the Lamb on the throne will be their Shepherd. He will lead them to springs of life-giving water. And God will wipe every tear from their eyes.' Here Jesus, the Lamb of God, is also the Shepherd and the one who has safely led his people to the place of eternal security and blessing.

As with the other portraits of God, this image of God as our guide is not just for us to stand back and admire. It is for us to imitate. We are to be guides ourselves. Imagine that, while driving down some cliff-top road, someone urgently waved you to a stop and pointed out that the road ahead had collapsed into the sea. As you returned along the road, grateful for your escape from near disaster, wouldn't you feel obliged to pass on the news to other drivers heading the same way? Followers of Jesus are to do all we can to warn those on the wrong road, and to direct them to the right one.

16

THE GOD WHO **TRANSFORMS US**

God wants to rescue, forgive, adopt and guide us. Yet there is a desire God has that is perhaps even more astonishing than any of these – he desires to *transform* us. The Bible reveals that the God who desires us to walk the way with him is not content to let us remain as we are. He wants to change us into beings who are perfect in every way.

The desire to be changed is universal. Almost everyone, sooner or later, feels dissatisfied with who they are. Everywhere, men and women wish they could resist temptation – and be happier, more joyful and more content. Everybody, it seems, wants to be a 'better person'. The hope of personal transformation lies at the heart of all religion. Yet, what the Bible teaches on this subject is very different from what other religions teach. While almost all religions suggest, 'Transform yourself and you might meet God,' Christianity says the very reverse: 'Come to God through Jesus and he will transform you.' In Christianity, our transformation is not the *cause* of us meeting with God; it is the *effect* of God meeting with us. Christianity is the faith of *grace*: the principle that God comes off the throne and comes down to help people who do not, in any way, deserve his kindness.

So how does God transform and change those who come to him? And into what are they changed? At first glance, the Old Testament appears to say little about the need for transformation; its emphasis seems to lie with doing right actions. Yet there is also an awareness that the problem of the human race lies deeper than actions and that the great human need is for internal transformation. The prophets looked forward to a day when God would work such a radical and deep-seated change in people's lives. So, in Ezekiel 36:26–27 we hear God promising, 'And I will give you a new heart, and I will put a new spirit in you. I will take out your stony, stubborn heart and give you a tender, responsive heart. And I will put my Spirit in you.' The meaning of these words is illustrated in the next chapter by a remarkable vision of a valley of dry, lifeless bones, which, under the breath of the Holy Spirit, come alive. It is a dramatic image of how God takes those who are spiritually dead and makes them alive. There are other passages that teach that God's desire is not for a people who follow him by keeping laws and performing rituals, but for people who are transformed internally by his Spirit.

It is Jesus, though, who shifts the focus entirely away from external actions to being transformed by God. He pointed out that the problem of life was not just that we do wrong actions, it was that – deep down – we have the wrong attitudes. Jesus' radical diagnosis came with a suitably radical prescription. There has to be a total internal transformation, a change of life – a *conversion*. Jesus told a religious leader, 'I tell you the truth, unless you are born again, you cannot see the Kingdom of God,' and went on to talk of the need to be 'born of the Spirit' (John 3:1–5). These demands appear to be impossible. After all, how do we change what we are deep down? Yet, here and elsewhere in his teaching, Jesus put himself forward as the one who can bring about such a total change. On the one hand, Jesus insisted on a total transformation; on the other, he claimed he could make such a transformation occur. He made the demand and, at the same time, offered to fulfil it.

The letters of the New Testament bubble over with the excitement that, with Jesus, transformation is possible. They are full of references to 'having a new life', 'being made a new creation', 'having a new relationship with God', 'being brought into God's family' and moving from 'life to death'. Paul summarises the transformation this way: 'This means that anyone who belongs to Christ has become a new person. The old life is gone; a new life has begun!' (2 Corinthians 5:17).

God wants to change us, but into what? The awesome answer is that God intends us to be *like Christ*. Paul tells us that 'God knew his people in advance, and he chose them to become like his Son, so that his Son would be the firstborn among many brothers and sisters' (Romans 8:29). We are not just adopted into the family of Jesus and allowed to remain who we are. Instead, God intends that we will, sooner or later, bear a resemblance to Jesus Christ, our elder brother.

It is helpful to realise that there are three aspects to this transformation: past, present and future. In the *past*, the follower of Jesus is someone who has already been transformed – at conversion they have been rescued, forgiven and adopted. They are like some old, crumbling, rundown building that has been purchased by someone intent on renovating it. The really important and fundamental change has already taken place: they are now under new management.

In the *present*, the follower of Jesus is also someone who is being transformed. To extend our building image, God's renovation work on them is underway. Every Christian is a 'work in progress'. A sculptor once explained how he had made a statue of a lion by simply removing everything from the block of stone that was not part of the lion; in the same way, God removes everything from our lives that doesn't look like Christ. Many followers of Jesus find that the idea that God is working to transform them helps them to understand the struggles that they undergo – in the problems they suffer, they see God chipping off things in their lives that are not Christ-like.

However, the greatest aspect of the transformation lies ahead of us, in the *future*. Paul speaks of it like this: 'And we eagerly await a Saviour from there, the Lord Jesus Christ, who, by the power that enables him to bring everything under his control, will transform our lowly bodies so that they will be like his glorious body' (Philippians 3:20–21, NIV). One day, the Bible teaches, we will finally be completely transformed. To return to our building image, however unfinished and untidy things may seem at the moment, we can be confident about the future. We have caught a glimpse of God's plans and they are glorious.

Three important points need a brief mention. First, although the word *transform* is an accurate one, it could be misleading if you thought that it meant that God wanted to change you into something strange or alien. In fact, God's transformation is more of a restoration. He is working to restore us to what we would have been if we hadn't rebelled against him – we are being changed, not into something that is *less* human, but into something that is *more* human. After all, if Jesus was the perfect human, to become more like him is to become more like what we ought to be.

Second, although the task of transforming us may seem an impossible one, we need to remember that this is God's work and he has all the power that is needed. Paul says this: 'I also pray that you will understand the incredible greatness of God's power for us who believe him. This is the same mighty power that raised Christ from the dead and seated him in the place of honour at God's right hand in the heavenly realms' (Ephesians 1:19–20). Here, Jesus' resurrection is simultaneously an example of God's transforming power and the proof that our own transformation will ultimately happen. Furthermore, as with God's other actions towards us, the Holy Spirit is involved. Again, Paul wrote, 'The Spirit of God, who raised Jesus from the dead, lives in you. And just as God raised Christ Jesus from the dead, he will give life to your mortal bodies by this same Spirit living within you' (Romans 8:11).

Third, our transformation is not automatic. Yes, God takes the initiative in rescuing, forgiving and adopting us and, through his Spirit, gives us the power to change, but we must co-operate with him in our transformation. Paul expresses it like this: 'Dear friends, you always followed my instructions when I was with you. And now that I am away, it is even more important. Work hard to show the results of your salvation, obeying God with deep reverence and fear. For God is working in you, giving you the desire and the power to do what pleases him' (Philippians 2:12–13). Here there is the perfect balance – God has saved us and given us the power to do what pleases him, but we must obey him in order that our transformation is put 'into action'. In fact, the process by which we are transformed may well be hard work. Think of someone who is completely unfit turning themselves into an Olympic-class athlete; it is going to be a painful process of transformation. The change to being like Christ is just as radical, just as demanding, but ultimately will be infinitely more rewarding.

Finally, we have seen how these 'portraits of God' are also our patterns, in that how God acts is an example for us. The way in which Christ transforms his people is no exception: his followers are to be those who delight in being agents of transformation. The resurrected Jesus said this to his disciples, 'As the Father has sent me, I am sending you' (John 20:21, NIV). We are to be those people whose desire is to do what Jesus did – to transform the lives of others and of our world for good. Jesus said, 'My purpose is to give them a rich and satisfying life' (John 10:10) and those who follow him are to bring life into their world.

The idea that God desires to utterly transform us, in a way that is beyond our imagining, is so awesome that it should give Jesus' followers hope and encouragement even during the darkest times of their lives. 'One day,' we can say with confidence, 'I will be changed!' The idea that God wants to transform us should arouse not just praise and gratitude but also awe, excitement and expectancy.

17

THE GOD WHO REQUIRES
A RESPONSE

We have seen five portraits of how God acts towards his people. We have seen how he *rescues* us, *forgives* us, *adopts* us, *guides* us and *transforms* us. It is worth remembering that these are not abstract ideas – they are things that God quite literally 'fleshed out' in Jesus Christ. The New Testament says this of Jesus: 'The Son radiates God's own glory and expresses the very character of God' (Hebrews 1:3). In other words, if we want to know what it means, in practical terms, for God to be the one who rescues, forgives, adopts, guides and transforms, we can look at Jesus.

Two questions may have arisen and need considering. The first is this: which of these five pictures of God in action is the most important? Are we to think of God primarily as rescuer, forgiver, adopter, guide or transformer? The answer is that all of these are important and for us to lose sight of any of them would be to give us a distorted view of God. In fact, many of the divisions in Christianity have occurred precisely because there has been an inability to balance all these different images of who God is and what he does. So, for example, someone who sees God only as a forgiver may feel that someone who thinks of him, more or less exclusively, as a rescuer is mistaken, and vice versa. We need to keep *all five* images in view. These different portraits of God, taken together, give a great breadth and depth to our knowledge and understanding of God.

The second question follows on from this: if each portrait is valid, which is the best one to start with? Traditionally, followers of Jesus have said that it is vital that, first of all, we come to know God as our forgiver. After all, they say, our sins have made a barrier between us and God and have to be dealt with. This is absolutely right, and is the pattern that many people experience when they undergo conversion to Jesus Christ. Yet many people who become followers of Jesus do not experience this pattern. Sometimes they seem to experience God first as rescuer, guide and transformer or even as the one who adopts them and, only later, do they come to see God as the one who forgives them. In other words, it seems that the order in which people come to understand and appreciate these different aspects of God varies. Perhaps the wisest thing that can be said is that, as soon as possible, those who have become Christians should seek to know God in every aspect of his personality.

Yet important as these questions are, there is a more pressing issue. The fact is that all these aspects of God demand a *response*. It is as if God is saying, 'This is who I am. This is what I desire to do in your life. Now, what are you going to do about it?' There can be no place for the disinterested observer who coolly examines these aspects of God, nods wisely and then, quite unaffected, moves on. Knowing facts about God is not enough. As the apostle James remarked, 'You believe that there is one God. Good! Even the demons believe that – and shudder' (James 2:19, NIV). When God reveals to us who he is, there ought to be a response. An appropriate three-stage response could be summed up in three words: acceptance, trust and obedience.

Acceptance means recognising and agreeing that what is stated is correct. Imagine someone who is told, as they drive across country, that they are going the wrong way and need to find a new route. Acceptance here would be for them to acknowledge that they were going the wrong way and that they need to change direction. In the case of these five portraits of God, acceptance is to acknowledge that they are true pictures of who God is. But it is also to admit that they require a personal response. So, to accept the idea of God being a rescuer is to say, 'Yes, I see that God is a rescuer and I also see that I *personally* need rescuing.'

Trust goes further than acceptance and means agreeing to take action based on a belief. It is to say, 'I agree that this is true, I see that it has implications for me and I am going to take the action that is needed.' To pursue the illustration of being lost, moving from acceptance to trust would mean agreeing to take the alternative directions offered. With God, to trust him is to say to him, 'I believe in who you are and I want to follow you.'

Obedience goes one step further still. It is to act on the basis of acceptance and belief. So, to return to the illustration of getting lost on a road, obedience is to actually take the new route. Similarly, to be obedient to God is to accept him as Lord of who we are and agree that he – and not we – will be in control from now on. It is important to remember that obedience is often a long-term process rather than a one-off action. Being obedient to the new driving instructions means not just setting off in that direction but keeping going in that direction. And to be obedient to God means more than just saying 'yes' to him at one moment in your life – it means keeping close to him ever afterwards.

It is important to recognise the existence of these three stages and the need for all of them. Many people get stuck at one of the first two stages. They may accept that Jesus is who they need, but they do not really get to the point of trusting him. They may trust in God in some abstract way, but fail to act in obedience to him – they believe *in* God but do not believe God. It is vital to decide to follow Jesus and to follow through that decision with action. Making the decision to follow Jesus is like turning the ignition key in a car. It is a small, almost insignificant, action but one that starts much greater processes going. But it is a decision that has to be made: without it, you go nowhere.

We need to recognise that people's experiences of becoming a follower of Jesus vary. Some have a sudden and dramatic experience of conversion, while for others coming to walk with Jesus is a slow and gradual process. The differences between the two may not be that significant. It's a bit like realising that you are driving down a road in the wrong direction. Whether you do a tyre-squealing U-turn or a leisurely three-point turn is not ultimately that important: it's the fact that you turn around and start heading in the right direction that matters.

The great command that God issued through Micah hints at this need to properly and personally respond to who God is. The call there was 'to act justly, to love kindness and to walk humbly with your God'. It could have simply been 'walk humbly with God' but it isn't; it is 'walk humbly with *your* God'. That little word 'your' makes all the difference. It speaks of ownership, possession and close relationship. It marks the difference between theoretical knowledge about someone and personal knowledge of them. To walk with someone – anyone – requires that we know them personally. We must have a personal relationship with God before we can walk with him.

We have seen in these chapters how God is the one who desires to rescue, forgive, adopt, guide, protect and transform us. The ultimate issue is not whether we believe that this is true as a general statement – it is whether we know it is true for us personally. We need to go from being able to say, 'I know that God forgives,' to saying, 'I know that God has forgiven me.' The first statement is like receiving a cheque; the second is like cashing it.

Sadly, it is possible to reject God. We might wish that it was impossible, that every road led back to him and that wherever we went and whatever we chose to do, God would, at the last, bring us back to himself. Yet the Bible teaches otherwise. In giving us freedom, God allows men and women to turn away from his outstretched hands of welcome and to choose to walk off on their own. But to walk away from the one who is the only rescuer, forgiver and guide is to make the very worst and most tragic of all choices. It is to choose darkness instead of light, sorrow instead of joy and death instead of life.

And what if we have been followers of Jesus for some time? How are we to respond to these pictures or images of who God is? Can they be ignored by those who are on the way? Of course not! All Christians, even those who have walked with God for many years, need to continually broaden and deepen their knowledge of God. Over time and under the stresses and strains of busy lives, it is all too easy to focus on only a few aspects of God. We may, for instance, begin to think of God only as the one who forgives or guides us, and neglect his other attributes. Yet there is much to be said for working at having a broader view of God – perhaps spending more time on those portraits of him that we are less familiar with. But breadth alone is not enough: we also need to seek depth in our understanding and experience of God's character and actions. The portraits of God drawn for us in the Bible are, like all great portraits, worthy of repeated and deep study. There are such depths to them that, even after a lifetime's study, new details or aspects will emerge. You never know all there is to know of God.

We have seen that God is the one who desires to *rescue*, *forgive*, *adopt*, *guide*, *protect* and *transform* us. When it comes to what God wants of us, the appropriate response to such a God ought to be as rich and varied as the portraits themselves – we should be filled with thankfulness, wonder and joy.

CONTINUING TO **WALK WITH GOD**

In responding to the question, 'What does God want of us?' we have so far looked at what it means to 'act justly' and to 'love kindness' and also what the characteristics are of the God with whom we should 'walk humbly'. In the previous section we also looked at how we should respond to the God who desires to help us along the way of life. We can call that action – of beginning the walk with God – many things: 'conversion', 'becoming a Christian', 'being born again' or 'becoming a child of God'. These are all overlapping and balancing descriptions of what has happened. Of course, the really important thing is not what you call this change, it is that this change has actually taken place. Now, in this final section, we consider how, having come to God in Christ, we continue to walk with him along the way of life – how our lives can be shaped by doing what God wants of us.

There is no seven-step programme to walking with God and there are two reasons why not. The first is that God, although an infinite and all-powerful being, is a person. He is not a force to be tapped, a condition to be achieved or a technique to be mastered – he is someone whom we are to relate to. The Bible speaks of how God is personal and how he wants a personal bond with those who follow him. The very reason we were made in God's image was so that we might have the potential to relate to God. Micah's call for his contemporaries 'to walk humbly with your God' uses the image of two people walking together. God wants a relationship with us, and relationships cannot be programmed or made the subject of a formula.

The second reason a simple programme will not work is that everyone is unique. Think of Mary and Max, two people who have both just decided to follow Jesus. Mary is a woman in her sixties who, by most people's standards, has 'got everything together': she is happily married, self-confident and financially secure. She is even a fairly moral person and, after a lifetime of attending church as a bystander, knows her way around the Bible. Max is very different. In his twenties, he is in a job that he hates, drinks more than is good for him and, after a string of failed relationships, considers that he is an almost total failure in life. He knows nothing whatever about the Bible and very little about God. Yet he, as well as Mary, has just come to Jesus and started to walk the right way. It is not hard to see that the needs of Mary and Max are very different. Clearly, one size does not fit all!

Yet, for Mary and Max – and in fact for all of us – there are general principles and guidelines that we can identify that will allow us to continue walking with God. But before we look at them, let's consider the challenges we face.

18

RECOGNISE **THE CHALLENGES**

The idea that, the moment we decide to walk with God, all our problems cease and our travelling through life is permanently free of trouble and full of happiness is extremely appealing. In reality, however, it has one fatal flaw: it just doesn't work. To promise that the way of life is now straightforward and painless is to mislead. The simple fact is that amid the undoubted joys and encouragements of being a Christian, the follower of Jesus will inevitably face many obstacles and challenges, some of which will be very tough.

Someone who has just become a follower of Jesus might ask why. 'After all,' they might protest, 'haven't I just acquired God as my Father, guide and protector? So why shouldn't my life be a gentle downhill stroll from now on?' It is a good question and the answer falls into two parts. First of all, the way of life that we walk along has not changed. Christian and non-Christian alike face the same difficulties: career issues, family crises, ill-health, bereavement and the like. The obstacles on the way remain and God seems to prefer to guide his children over such obstacles rather than remove them. But the second part of the answer is that when we become followers of Christ, two things do change – our relationship with God and our relationship with what we can, for the moment, simply call 'evil'. These two changes affect everything.

Let's consider our relationship with God first. We have already seen how one aspect of coming to God is knowing him as our Father and being adopted into his family. That has implications. In particular, our Father expects that we will adopt the family standards of behaviour and he is determined that one day we will be like Christ. In order to achieve that transformation God is prepared to use a range of methods. The result is the paradox that some of the challenges we face actually come from God himself. So, for instance, the new follower of Jesus may become aware that there are major areas of their life where change is required. Such changes may be widespread, fundamental and painful – the new Christian may find that hard action is required in connection with how they handle their finances, their love life or their work responsibilities. Yet it is God who wants these changes. Like the perfect parent that he is, God desires the best for us and wants us to grow up properly. As part of his care for us, God frequently exercises what parents call 'tough love', setting his children severe challenges and even imposing a loving discipline on them. His adoption of us as children requires nothing less. Remember: in order to mould his people, God often has to melt them.

Secondly, our relationship with evil has now changed. This is a complex area and needs careful consideration. We experience evil in our world in two basic ways: as a trend within us and as an external force. Within us, we find desires that seek to divert us from the right way. Although we would prefer to think of ourselves as people inclined to do good or, at worst, as morally neutral, the reality is that all human beings have an inbuilt tendency to desire – and do – what is wrong. So although we may decide that we are going to do what is right, in practice we gradually find that our actions have become compromised and in the end, what we actually do is something that falls far short of what we intended.

The traditional language for this is that human nature is 'sinful' and however unpopular, unfashionable and unflattering the term is, it explains a lot. The Bible teaches that this tendency towards the wrong thing is so deeply ingrained in all human beings that, although weakened, it persists beyond the process of conversion. Take, for instance, someone with a habit of flying into a rage who decides to follow Christ. Now, their conversion *may* take that habit away entirely. Many Christians can testify how, under the influence of God's Holy Spirit, some such troubling habit has vanished almost instantaneously. A more common pattern, however, would be for the tendency to fly into a rage to persist, but in a diluted form and as something that must be confronted on a regular basis. Eventually the follower of Jesus will learn to tame their temper. So as we seek to follow the way with God, our own internal attitudes may act as a continuing source of pressure and conflict upon us.

The Bible also identifies external influences towards evil. It teaches that the societies and cultures that we live in ('the world') are not neutral but are, like our minds, twisted away from good. In other words, the way of life does not run across a 'level playing field' but across one that is tilted and uneven.

Our experience confirms both these truths: we encounter pressures at every level to do the wrong thing – to choose what is convenient rather than what is correct, to pursue what is popular instead of what is good and to take the easy road instead of the right one. Yet the Bible goes deeper still – identifying, behind both these internal and external pressures towards doing what is wrong, the power and influence of the devil. This personal and supernatural hostility adds an extra dimension to the challenges that followers of Christ must face. From having been under the devil's authority they now belong to Christ and, having changed sides, are now subject to the devil's hostility. Now, of course, it is possible to over-emphasise the devil's presence and to blame him for everything, but underestimating him is unwise. Most Christians, especially when they have seriously tried to follow God over some difficult matter, have sensed at times the existence of a destructive and hostile personality opposing them.

It is important to remember that while the devil has a strictly limited power over the Christian – he has, after all, been defeated by Christ – the power he has can be used to considerable effect. The wise emphasis of the Bible is not on engaging in direct personal warfare with the devil but, instead, is on resisting and combating his schemes. These schemes tend to be variations on a few themes. It is worth being aware of three of these.

In popular belief, the main strategy the devil uses is of *direct attack*, letting loose on the follower of Jesus some sudden catastrophe or overpowering temptation. The idea is that, having been struck by an awful tragedy or having fallen into some appalling sin, the follower of Jesus then decides to give it all up. The reality is that such direct attacks seem to be less effective than might be imagined. Tragedies can turn people *to* God, instead of *away from* him and spectacular sins can produce remarkable repentance.

Other more subtle strategies occur. One is for us to be so *distracted* that we lose the way. What happens here is that, over time, other things come to seem more attractive so that slowly – and often without any major warning – we are led away from going in the right direction. The twist here is that the things that distract us are often good things. So something that is perfectly worthwhile (perhaps seeking promotion, keeping fit or being involved in some social initiative) gradually creeps in on our lives and acquires the absolute priority that following God should take. Without noticing, we have become distracted and are now heading down a side road that, although appearing at first to run parallel to the way, ultimately leads to a very different place. The answer to this specific temptation of distraction is to develop healthy habits that help us to stay focused on walking with God. Good friends and fellowships can also help us here.

The other subtle strategy is for us to be so *discouraged* that we give up on the way. This can be particularly effective and there are very few Christians who are immune from it. The pattern is well known: Christians start to walk with God with the very highest hopes and intentions but, after a while, they realise that they are falling short of their goals. Now the devil appears as an accuser (a title he has in the Bible) and reminds them of the gap between what they are supposed to be – a triumphant and glorious child of God – and the struggling and definitely un-glorious person that they feel that they are. He suggests that they may as well give up; they have failed. Their discouragement now shifts to despair. Curiously, it is precisely those people who aim highest who are most affected by discouragement. If you once had hopes of making the world a better place, finding out that you can't even stop the gossip in your office can be particularly discouraging! The specific answer to discouragement is to remember the great principle of grace – that God cares and loves us so much that, if we confess our sins to him and seek to turn from them, he will forgive. It has been said that our greatest mistake is not that we fall, but that we do not rise every time we fall.

These are specific challenges to the Christian life so how should they be approached? Part of the answer lies in developing wise attitudes. After all, how you live is determined not so much by what life brings to you as by the attitude you bring to life. So, for example, it is a good rule to realise that challenges to walking with God are inevitable and to be prepared for them. Perhaps the most important attitude to have is a determination to keep going, whether we feel like it or not.

Perhaps the wisest attitude of all is to develop what might be called 'good practices'. In the following chapters, we will look at five of these essentials for the Christian life. Each will help us to do what we have to do and to act justly, to love kindness and to walk humbly with our God.

19

ESSENTIAL 1:
UNDERSTANDING GOD:
READING THE BIBLE

The Bible provides at least five things for the follower of Jesus. These can be summarised as: information, instruction, illumination, illustration and inspiration. The combined effect of these is to help us understand more of who God is and what he wants for us. But before we look at these, it's worth thinking about what we hold in our hands when we pick up a Bible. What we have is a library of 66 books, written originally in Hebrew, Aramaic and Greek. The library includes history, poetry, letters, prayers, visions and even a love poem, written over a period of at least 1,000 years, by different authors in different cultures. Yet despite the various origins of these documents, Christians believe that God's Holy Spirit supervised their writing and collection, so that the Bible that resulted is God's word: it is what he wants to say to us. Christians also believe that the work of God's Spirit did not end with the collection of these books but continues, so that when the Bible is read, God speaks through it. Such views are not just theory – you could fill whole libraries with accounts of people and entire cultures that have been transformed by the reading of the Bible.

But do we need God's word in written form? After all, God can speak to people through feelings, or even dreams and visions – aren't these enough? The problem is that such things are intensely personal and can be distorted by an overactive imagination or wishful thinking. In contrast, a book is something that is fixed. Certainly, throughout history, people have found having God's word written down in a form that they can read, preserve and share has proved to be vital. To use again the image of the road, most drivers will have had the experience of being given a series of directions and then getting totally lost and wishing they had written the instructions down. The Bible is God's word set down securely in print so that we don't get lost on the way.

HOW THE BIBLE FUNCTIONS

Let's consider what the Bible provides.

Information. The Bible gives facts. Remarkably, for a book with such diverse origins, it traces a single great story – the relationship between God and human beings. The Bible begins with the creation of the universe and the disastrous rebellion of the human race against God. It then tells, in the rest of the Old Testament, how God began his rescue of humanity by calling out a race of people to whom he revealed something of himself and his standards. The New Testament starts with four accounts of the life, teaching and death on the cross of Jesus. It makes three astonishing and unique claims about Jesus: first, that he was God in human form; second, that he rose from the dead; and, third, that his death was a sacrifice for our sins. The rest of the New Testament explains how the good news of Jesus spread, giving rise to a new people of God drawn from all races and cultures, and it describes the implications of what he did for the lives of his followers. Amid echoes of the opening pages of the Old Testament, the New Testament ends with a wonderful vision of a restored humanity in a renewed universe.

Because the Bible is concerned with the story of how God rescues people, it has a very different perspective to what we might call 'ordinary history' and has only a limited concern with rulers and empires. It does, however, reveal the supernatural dimension to events. So, while history tells us that, in the sixth century BC, the Jewish nation was taken into exile in Babylon, it is only from the Bible that we learn that the ultimate cause of this traumatic event was their rebellion against God.

Yet the Bible also gives information about much more than history. It goes behind the scenes of life to tell us things that we would never otherwise know about. So, although we might have guessed something about what God is like from the world around us, only the Bible gives us reliable data about him. We also learn about ourselves, that we are not just physical beings but that we also have a spiritual dimension to our lives.

Instruction. The Bible gives instruction on how we are to live and provides us with warnings, encouragement and advice. In its pages we see the three great standards of how to live that we considered in the first section: the common values of all human beings; the Ten Commandments; and, above all, the life of Jesus Christ – God become one of us. Not all the instruction in the Bible is equally relevant to us. Some of the Old Testament laws applied specifically to a culture that no longer exists and others, such as those to do with temple worship, are now obsolete. Because the coming of Jesus changed everything, it is the New Testament that provides the fullest instructions for how God's people are to live today. Surrounded as we are in the twenty-first century by a sea of alternative advice on how to live, the importance of the Bible's instructions for us cannot be overestimated.

Illumination. The Bible can also be considered as light for our lives. Its teaching casts a light into the darkness of life and helps us to see where we are going. As a verse in the Psalms says, 'Your word is a lamp to guide my feet and a light for my path' (Psalm 119:105). When faced with difficulties in life, careful and prayerful consideration of the Bible's teaching is able to point out both hidden hazards and a safe way to walk.

Illustration. All good teachers use illustrations to demonstrate the practical importance of what is being taught. The Bible is no different: its pages are filled with illustrations and examples of how human beings succeed or fail at walking the way with God. So, for example, the Bible doesn't just teach about the dangers of lust or pride, it gives illustrations that show just what happens if such things do take a hold of our life. In places, the illustrations do not just supplement the instruction – they *are* the instruction. So, for instance, instead of telling us in enormous detail what we must do to live up to God's perfect standards, the Bible shows us the life of Jesus. There we see, far more effectively than in any list of dos and don'ts, exactly what it means to live as a follower of God.

Inspiration. It is common to talk about the Bible being inspired by God and of course it is. But in another sense it is also a source of inspiration. It is very easy to rationalise what the Bible is and to see it simply as a series of statements that we must agree with. Yet there is more to the Bible than this. In its words, there is a life and a power than cannot be explained away. The Bible can comfort, console and challenge us in a way that no other book can. It is not just the written record of God's message to us; it is also a channel through which God continues to speak to us today.

USING THE BIBLE

The Bible should be widely used in Christian life. All church services should include some time where a part of the Bible is explained or applied and, in addition to this, many followers of Jesus have found that the study of the Bible in small groups is invaluable. Yet, traditionally, the main place where the Christian encounters God's word is in the private and personal study of the Bible.

So how, practically, are we to read the Bible? There are several helpful principles.

Read regularly. Like vitamins, the Bible needs to be taken regularly for best effect. The traditional practice of setting aside some time every day to read the Bible is wise.

Read confidently. In order for the Bible to benefit our lives, the best attitude is undoubtedly confident trust that it is God's written word for us. Of course, there are technical issues – the dating and authorship of different books of the Bible, the exact meaning of words – but the universal experience of Christians is that such issues are best not pursued in the time one gives to private Bible reading and study. Our priority is to feed on God's word, not to analyse it.

Read expectantly. It is a good policy to come to the Bible expecting that, as God caused it to be written in the past, he will speak through it today. To open a Bible with an attitude that it will have nothing to say to you is almost certainly a self-fulfilling prophecy.

Read wisely. The meaning of most of the Bible is straightforward but there are some guidelines that can help.

- Use an up-to-date translation. However splendid and majestic some of the older versions may sound, the Bible was meant to be read in contemporary language. There are many good modern versions, such as the New Living Translation (NLT) or the New International Version (NIV) that are easier to understand.

- Be sensitive to the context and style of the passage. For instance, to read a piece of poetry as history (or vice versa) is to distort its meaning.

- Don't get hung up on hard bits. Mark Twain remarked it was not the bits of the Bible that he didn't understand that worried him – it was the bits that he did. Yes, there are tricky passages in the Bible but they are rarely critical ones. As a rule, when it comes to important issues, we find that the Bible speaks plainly and in more than one place. Where you do find a difficulty, remember that you are most unlikely to be the first person to have faced it, so consult some of the many good resources that are available, such as study guides and Bible commentaries.

Read completely. Make a point of reading the entire Bible, not just selected parts. It is a good rule that 'the Bible interprets itself' so that a passage in one place will be explained in another. We need to be open to hear the whole Word of God, not just selected parts of it. To read the Bible on a hit or miss basis will almost certainly guarantee that you miss more than you hit.

Read prayerfully. The Bible and prayer go together. The same Holy Spirit that supervised the writing of the Bible is the one who God promises will be with all who believe in Jesus. In other words, we do not just have access to the word of God, we also have access to the author. Prayer helps us, both in the interpretation of God's word and in the application of it to our lives.

Read reflectively. If at all possible, our reading of the Bible should not be done hastily: there should be time to reflect on what the Bible says to us. Reading the Bible without reflecting on it is like trying to eat without swallowing. We may find, as others have, that the mirror of God's word is sometimes painfully clear. There should be a determination to apply what God is saying in his word to our lives. We are not meant to be unchanged by reading God's word and, when we read it, we must always ask ourselves such questions as:

- What have I learned here?

- How does this apply to me?

- How, as result of reading this, should I change my life?

- What promises are there for me to take hold of?

- What instructions are there for me to obey?

Read obediently. A final rule is that, when we read God's word, we ought always to be prepared to obey what we find in it. The Bible is not meant merely to inform, but to transform. Obedience is the key that opens the door to understanding, disobedience locks it shut. Our great need is almost always not to have more knowledge; it is to put into practice what we already know. To know the will of God is the greatest knowledge, but to do the will of God is the greatest achievement.

We will never fully understand who God is. After all, he is God: infinite, eternal and magnificent beyond anything we can imagine. Yet God has bent down and revealed all we need to know about himself in the Bible. By studying God's word, we will come to understand both who he is and who we are.

20

ESSENTIAL 2:
COMMUNICATING WITH GOD: 1
THE PURPOSE AND PRACTICE OF PRAYER

Why do we pray? There are four reasons. The first is so that God himself is honoured and given glory. Yes, God is already King and Lord over the entire universe but in prayer we ask that this reality is revealed to the world. We are praying, in effect, 'Lord, act so that people see who you are.' The second reason is that, in prayer, we are bringing requests for God to answer. The Bible teaches that, like the perfect Father that he is, God delights to hear and answer our requests. Remember: when we work, we work, but when we pray, God works. A third purpose of prayer is to enable us to become more like God. You are more likely to become like someone if you spend time in their presence. As a part of helping us become more like Christ, prayer has an especially important role in helping us overcome temptation. A fourth purpose of prayer is to show love to others by bringing God's healing and saving power into troubled lives or situations. Through prayer, we are able to help others and play our part in God's purposes for this world.

A key part of walking with anybody is communication. How can you have any sort of a relationship and not communicate? The means by which we communicate with God is prayer. Personal prayer lies at the very heart of 'walking with God' – prayer is the means by which we begin, maintain and develop our relationship with God.

PRAYER BEGINS OUR RELATIONSHIP WITH GOD

The starting point in the Christian life is the very first prayer to God in which we ask for forgiveness and declare that we want to become one of Jesus' followers. It is the equivalent, in words, of you putting your hand into God's outstretched hand.

PRAYER MAINTAINS OUR RELATIONSHIP WITH GOD OUR FATHER

Any relationship between two people needs communication and the relationship between God and one of his children is no different. Prayer is basically talking to God; it is through prayer that we thank our heavenly Father for what he has done for us, share our concerns with him, ask his forgiveness and seek his wisdom. Some people pray only in a crisis – yet true prayer is a way of life, not just something for emergency use.

PRAYER DEEPENS OUR RELATIONSHIP WITH GOD

It is through prayer that we are enabled to understand more of who God is and what he wants for us. In an age preoccupied with activity and achievements, prayer may seem insignificant. Yet it is not. Prayer is vital and the simplest measure of any Christian's state of spiritual health is the quality of his or her prayer life. Prayer is the key to the contentment, peace and joy that God wants all his children to have. It is hard to see how any followers of Jesus can be either happy or effective for any length of time unless they are regularly talking to their heavenly Father in prayer. Prayer is the great essential in the life of a follower of Jesus. It is possible to imagine Christians who, perhaps because of their isolation, never attend a church or read a Bible but it is not possible to imagine one who never prays.

Yet if prayer is vital to how we walk with God, it is also badly understood. Today there are various ideas about what prayer is, many of them derived from religions other than Christianity. Yet Christian prayer is distinctively different, not just because of the involvement of God the Father, God the Son and God the Holy Spirit in our prayers but also because Christian prayer works differently. Six distinctive elements mark Christian prayer:

- Christian prayer is marked by *reality*. While there is a mystery to prayer, praying is not the mystical pursuit of some unknown god or spirit or 'spiritual' state of mind. God has revealed himself in the Bible and, above all, in Jesus Christ. We know the person to whom we pray and our prayers should reflect this.

- Christian prayer is marked by a sense of *relationship*. Fundamental to all praying is the fact that prayer is communicating with God our Father. Prayer is not engaging in a magic ritual, it is talking to God as our heavenly parent.

- Christian prayer is marked by a sense of *release* from regulations. Because it is the expression of a relationship, there is freedom. There is no need to pray at a specific time, in a specific way or using a specific set of words.

- Christian prayer is marked by a sense of *reassurance*. The God of the Bible invites prayer; he delights in it. Equally, because Jesus Christ offers forgiveness, any feelings of guilt can and should be dealt with. The hallmark of Christian praying is confidence.

- Christian prayer is marked by a sense of *rejoicing*. God has made a way for us to know him by rescuing, forgiving and adopting us. That is an extraordinary basis for joy!

- Finally, Christian prayer should be marked by a desire to *respond*. Prayer is something that ought to overflow into our lives. We need to walk away from having prayed with a new vision of who God is and how we can serve him. Prayer doesn't just change things – it should change us.

So how do we pray? Here, as elsewhere, the Bible is full of both instruction and illustration. Prayers, and praying people, occur throughout the Bible. In the Old Testament, the book of Psalms is an entire book of different kinds of prayers. In the New Testament, Jesus is the supreme example of someone whose life was centred around prayer. In what we call the 'Lord's Prayer' (Matthew 6:9–13), Jesus even made a point of giving his disciples a pattern prayer to follow. The letters of the New Testament are full of prayers, references to prayers and instructions to pray. From these, and from the wisdom of other followers of Jesus over the centuries, we can find guidelines about the practice of prayer.

WHEN SHOULD WE PRAY?

The basic answer is often and regularly. Many Christians pray at the start and end of every day and make time for longer prayer at whichever time is most suitable for them. It is a good rule not to face the day until you have faced God.

HOW SHOULD WE PRAY?

In keeping with the idea that prayer is communication with our heavenly Father, most followers of Jesus use whatever words come to them, rather than fixed prayers. The posture adopted for prayer varies and, while most people pray silently, some find that it helps their concentration to pray aloud. Normally, prayers are made to God the Father in the name (that is, through the authority) of Jesus Christ. Even here, though, there is some variation and prayers to Jesus occur in the New Testament.

WHERE SHOULD WE PRAY?

God is everywhere so you can pray anywhere. There is an extraordinary freedom in Christian prayer: people pray anywhere that is convenient, preferably where they can be quiet and undisturbed. But location is no barrier to prayer – some people even make a point of praying on their journey to work.

WHAT CAN HELP US TO PRAY EFFECTIVELY?

Most followers of Jesus link at least some of their praying with Bible reading, perhaps letting what they have read flow over into their prayers. Some keep a prayer list to remind them whom and what they ought to pray for. Another aid to prayer is to keep a notebook in which specific prayers are noted along with the answers when they occur. This not only builds faith, it also develops a focused attitude to praying.

There are many issues to do with prayer, but they should never ever obscure the one key fact – we need to pray.

21

ESSENTIAL 3:
COMMUNICATING WITH GOD: 2
THE PATTERN OF PRAYER

Even if we limit ourselves to the subject of private prayer, we find that it includes various elements. So how should we pray? The best pattern for daily personal prayer seems to be to follow a cycle with the following elements: praise, confession, thanksgiving and requests with, in closing, a return to praise. Let's look at each element in turn.

PRAISE

To start prayer with praising God is good. To praise God is to celebrate all that he is – his goodness, justice, kindness and generosity. This sort of praise serves many functions but perhaps its main purpose is to put everything into perspective. It reminds us, at the very start of our praying, who God is and who we are. People often find that, after praising God, their problems no longer seem as overwhelming or as impossible as before. They have discovered that life's best outlook comes from a prayerful 'up look'.

Another advantage of praise is that, by reminding us of who God is, it helps prevent our prayers being totally concerned with ourselves. This makes sense – there is more to prayer than us getting our needs answered.

CONFESSION

To confess our sins and failings early on in our times of prayer is sensible. Prayer is communication and so is based on a relationship that, like any other, must be kept in a good state of repair. Sins that are not confessed to God are a barrier to effective prayer. So it is good to pause at the start of our time of prayer and ask God to show us what is wrong in our lives. If we can't think of anything here then we ought perhaps to look at our own lives in the light of Micah 6:8 and ask ourselves whether we have acted justly, loved kindness and walked humbly with God? Confessing reminds us that we can only come to God on the basis of grace. Nothing we have done gives us any automatic right to come to God: we all need forgiveness on a daily basis.

Yet we also need to go beyond confession – we need to seek and accept the forgiveness that God offers us in Jesus Christ. Here, the Lord's Prayer and other passages in the New Testament make an important point: we cannot ask for forgiveness for ourselves without also giving it to those who need it from us. Our failure to forgive others effectively blocks our own forgiveness.

THANKSGIVING

To give thanks is to remember what God has already done for us. Gratitude is an important element in any relationship, but here it is particularly vital – it reminds us that what God has done in the past he can do again.

REQUESTS

In thinking about the purpose of prayer, we saw that making requests to God was a very important element in prayer. God wants us to ask him for things, especially when our requests are wise and good. Concerning our own wants, it is worth remembering that God gives his very best to those who leave the choice with him. In practical terms, it may be helpful to think of praying in terms of a series of circular zones. So we may start with ourselves and our concerns, and then move out through our family and friends, before mentioning organisations and causes that we are concerned about. Finally, we may want to raise issues in the wider world. Where possible, specific requests are best but remember, when praying, don't give God instructions – he listens to prayer, not advice.

PRAISING AGAIN

It is not a good idea to let our prayers just tail away into silence as we run out of time or topics. A much better pattern is to end in a brief return to praise, so that praise acts like bookends to our prayers. That way, we remind ourselves again who God is and in doing so we let him, and not our problems, have the last word. To end with the little word *amen* is also important: it signifies our agreement with what we have prayed for.

Two other important aspects of prayer need mentioning. The first is that all the way through our praying we ought to be *listening*, expectantly prepared for God to speak to us. God may speak to us in various ways, perhaps by reminding us through his Holy Spirit of a Bible passage or by making us aware, in some other way, of his will. A second aspect of prayer is *taking action* based on prayer. Prayer is not just an end in itself – it should motivate action. After we have finished praying, we should carry out what God has put into our hearts and minds. Obedience is not only the key that opens the door to understanding the Bible, it is also the key to effective prayer. It is foolish to claim the promises of God without choosing to obey the commands of God.

Many people find that they have problems with some aspects of prayer. Let's look at three common obstacles to prayer.

First, *can we ask for the wrong thing?* Imagine a friend is applying for a new job and we really aren't sure that it is the best thing for them – how do we pray? We wouldn't want them to get it if it was the wrong job. Here we are helped by the fact that prayer does not automatically achieve whatever we ask; it is making requests to someone who is our perfect heavenly Father and who knows what the best answer is for those for whom we pray. So, even if, with the best of intentions, we were to ask for something that might not actually be the best for our friend we can trust that God will overrule. The idea that God can and will overrule our prayers gives us the freedom to pray confidently. Of course, this is no excuse for naïve or unwise prayers; it is always a good principle to pray in a thoughtful and intelligent manner. But so often we do not know what is right and here it is a relief to know that God does.

Second, *why is prayer unanswered?* Sometimes people's prayers are not answered because there is something wrong between them and God. The answering of requests in prayer is part of that two-way relationship that we have called 'walking with God'. Sadly, people sometimes want God to answer their prayers without walking with him. They simply want to come to him, grab what they want and run away again. Under such circumstances, it is hard to see how God can answer their prayers – to do so would only encourage such practices. Yet this does not explain all unanswered prayer. At other times, there is nothing wrong with the relationship with God but he still does not answer. Why not? Here we come back again to the idea that God is our heavenly Father. He knows far better than we do what is best for us, and he has his own all-wise agenda for our lives, an agenda that looks far beyond our current day-to-day concerns. So sometimes we ask for things without realising that, good though such things may be, God knows they are not in our best long-term interest. And when you realise that with God 'long term' extends to eternity, you can see why he refuses some requests.

It is also worth remembering that God isn't limited to answering 'yes' or 'no' to our requests. Sometimes, what we take to be a 'no' is actually something more subtle. In fact, God may be saying one of three things:

- 'Wait.' God's time is the best time and God's delays are not God's denials.

- 'Do it yourself.' Like the good Father that he is, God may encourage us to answer our own prayers.

- 'I have a better idea.' Here God is saying, in effect, 'I will answer your prayer but in a way that is very different from how you imagine.' This is the sort of answer where someone prays for a bicycle today but is given a car tomorrow instead. You might argue that it was unanswered prayer, but the recipient doesn't complain! God has simply changed the packaging on his blessing.

Third, *why does prayer seem a struggle*? We may find it hard to make time to pray, may find our minds unable to concentrate on prayer or may find God's presence elusive when we do pray. We are inclined to give in. What is happening? It may be an encouragement to know that all followers of Jesus have acknowledged that at times prayer can be an effort. We may want to blame the forces of evil for this – and as prayer lies at the heart of walking with God you can see why the devil might seek to disrupt it. The best advice is to try to be disciplined at prayer so that you persist in praying, whether you feel God's presence or not. Of course, he is never really absent – it just seems like it.

So far we have thought really only of private prayer and in the next chapter we will touch on public prayer as part of church worship. A third type of prayer exists – that which takes place in small groups. When two or more people gather for prayer, either for each other or for further concerns, the testimony of many Christians is that this can be very effective and can open the way to enormous blessing.

The importance of prayer cannot be over-emphasised. Because it is at the very heart of our relationship with God, we need to make prayer our main concern. If we are weak here, we are weak everywhere. With prayer, it is easy to be content with the merely adequate, but we should continue to work at developing and deepening our prayer life. When we think about the power, joy and peace that prayer releases in our own life and the lives of others it would be foolish not to give prayer the highest priority.

22

ESSENTIAL 4:
BEING IN COMMUNITY
WITH OTHERS:
FELLOWSHIP AND THE CHURCH

So far, when we have thought about walking with God we have considered issues almost entirely in terms of our individual walk with him. There is a lot of sense in doing this. After all, we must personally choose to follow God – no one else can do it for us. It is also important to realise that, as individuals, we are personally responsible for walking the way of life. Yet this view is only part of the picture, because the Bible teaches that we are not rescued by God to stay on our own – we are rescued to be part of a community, the Church. However, because for many people the practice of 'church' has such negative connotations, it is important that we look at the theory first and it is especially important to let the Bible, rather than our own experiences, define what it means by 'church'.

The idea that God wants to create not just new individuals, but a new people, is one of the great themes of the Bible. We see how God bends down to the world and draws out of it a people who will belong to him. The New Testament shows how, after the death and resurrection of Jesus, everybody – from whatever region or background – who finds Jesus as Saviour and Lord is made part of this new people of God. The New Testament ends with the vision of God's people enjoying eternal fellowship with him amid the new heavens and new earth.

We have already seen that anyone who puts their faith in Christ is adopted as a child of God and becomes part of God's family. In doing so they become part of what the New Testament calls 'the Church'. The idea here, though, is very different from most people's mental picture of the church as a building or a meeting. The word *church* has the sense of a people who are 'called out': they are those people whom God has reached down to and rescued, forgiven and adopted. The New Testament teaches that the Church lies at the heart of God's great plan for the world. Accordingly, it is given various amazing titles – for example, the body of Christ (1 Corinthians 12:12), the bride of Christ (Ephesians 5:25) and the household of God (1 Timothy 3:15). Every one of us who puts our faith in Jesus becomes part of this vast body of people, even if we have never met another follower of Jesus. We are no longer alone.

Why is it that this new community of the Church is so important? In the Bible we find the following answers:

- As God is Father, Son and Holy Spirit, he is effectively a community himself. The Church is, in some way, modelled on how God is.

- It is good for us to be in a community with others. We can help each other and be helped in turn because we are part of a family.

- Being in a community is vital for our spiritual development. The Church is a place of training, encouragement and – sometimes – rebuke. It is often the place where we get the rough edges rubbed off us.

- The existence of God's people is a powerful demonstration of the victory of Jesus Christ. One of the main goals of the devil is disintegration and he works hard towards discord, delighting in fragmenting families, societies and nations into hate-filled, warring elements. God's plan is the exact opposite: integration and unity, harmony and agreement. By triumphing over racial and cultural barriers, the Church should be the visible demonstration of God's purpose and power. The apostle Paul wrote that 'God's purpose in all this was to use the church to display his wisdom in its rich variety to all the unseen rulers and authorities in the heavenly places. This was his eternal plan, which he carried out through Christ Jesus our Lord' (Ephesians 3:10–11).

Yet although the New Testament lays down the theory of how, and why, Christians belong to the universal Church, its emphasis is much more down to earth. It is on how, practically, we are to live together as believers. The New Testament never sees the Church as a place but always as people. Also, the biblical Church did not occur once a week when individual followers of Jesus came together, it was a permanently existing Holy Spirit-bonded community that sometimes expressed itself in meetings. The believers might have lived in separate houses and come from different social backgrounds but there was an enormous, continuing and genuine unity between them. The New Testament Christians did not attend church: they *were* church.

So what, according to the New Testament, should a local church be doing? Jesus commanded only two specific practices. The first of these was baptism – the public ceremony marking someone's entry into the community of believers. The second was Holy Communion or the Lord's Supper – the regular and repeated commemoration of Jesus' death. However, beyond these, we can identify from the New Testament at least seven things that a church ought to be doing.

1. EXPRESSING WORSHIP

Perhaps the most important task of God's people is to express their gratitude and praise to God. The lives of

God's people, especially when they gather together, ought to be marked by joyful and reverent celebration of all that God is and all that he has done. Why?

First, we are to worship God because he deserves our worship. God is the maker of everything good – he deserves praise. Not to praise him would be unjust. Second, we are to worship so that we see our world in its right perspective. By reminding ourselves how great is the God with whom we walk, we see how insignificant the problems that threaten us on the way of life really are. It is as if, in celebrating God, we ascend a high mountain from which we are able to see everything more clearly, including the way of life. Third, we are to worship God because it protects us from worshipping other things. Human beings seem to be worshipping creatures and, if we do not worship God, we will worship something else. Sadly, there is no shortage of alternatives – material things, sex, political systems and even ourselves. All of these will harm us; worshipping God protects us from them.

There is an important point here – to worship is not primarily to meet together to sing hymns or songs. That may be part of worship, but it is far from all of it. Public worship should involve many things – praying, singing, Bible teaching and giving. But even that doesn't exhaust the meaning of worship. Quite simply, worship shouldn't be thought of as something that is confined to public gatherings on Sundays: it ought rather to be something that is permanently part of the lives of the followers of Jesus. Worship – declaring God's value and worth – ought to be part of everything we do. One person might decide to celebrate God by always doing their best work, another by working for justice, another by showing love to someone who would otherwise be neglected, and still another by stemming a tendency to criticism and gossip in their workplace. All, in their way, can be seen as ways of celebrating God. Paul summarised the principle as follows: 'Whether you eat or drink, or whatever you do, do it all for the glory of God' (1 Corinthians 10:31). Whether we work at home or manage a multinational corporation, we ought to do it in a way that celebrates God and what he has done. Acting justly and loving kindness is part of our worship.

2. PRACTISING FELLOWSHIP

The recurring theme of the New Testament is that at its heart a church should be a deep, real and loving fellowship. In the New Testament, Christians regularly ate together, shared in each other's joys and sorrows and helped each other out in every way possible. As God's adopted children, they recognised that they were part of new families and lived that out in what they did for each other. Thankfully, many churches today are attempting to recover this sense of close community.

3. INSTRUCTING IN TRUTH

The community of believers must be committed to learning more of what God wants for his people. Central to this should be the teaching of God's word, the Bible, either in preaching or in other ways, such as Bible studies. Such teaching, involving both the teaching of truth and the exposing of error, is always practical and applied, not just head knowledge.

4. ENCOURAGING HOLINESS

'Holiness' is an almost forgotten term these days, yet there is no other word that expresses as well the requirement that God's people should become like their heavenly Father in all things. The local church should be a place where what is right is encouraged and what is wrong is opposed, so there needs to be some sort of accountability and discipline structure within local church fellowships.

5. SHOWING LOVE

The relationships within the community of God's people are to be regulated by love. This is not simply the emotional feeling that is often called love today – it is a determined and sacrificial commitment to lovingly serve each other. Of course, this love is not just expressed in meetings, it is also expressed in day-to-day care for each other.

It is also shown in such down-to-earth matters as giving money. The command to act justly, to love kindness and to walk humbly with God doesn't just apply to individuals – it applies to churches.

6. DEMONSTRATING UNITY

Because unity already exists at a spiritual level, the Church community should aim to work out that oneness in practice and should be free from divisions of any sort – whether social, racial or cultural. In taking Holy Communion together, followers of Jesus commemorate the unity that they have with each other and with the crucified and resurrected Christ. *Unity* is not the same as *uniformity* – God doesn't want us all to become the same. The wisdom of God is seen in the way that people find unity in the Church without losing their distinctive individuality.

7. WITNESSING TO THE GOOD NEWS

These communities of God's people are not simply to be inward-looking 'holy huddles', they are also to look outwards. They are to declare and demonstrate what God has done in Jesus by letting what they are as fellowships spill out into the lives of those around them. Such witness to those around them is not simply to be in words – it should be in service and care.

These practices ought to mark the pattern of what a Christian fellowship is like. Inevitably, our churches often fail to live up to such a standard, with the result that some have rejected the existing church system outright, others put up with the substandard churches or drift around churches looking for the right one. Yet commitment to a church is vital, and sometimes the best place for us to be is where we are challenged rather than where we are comforted. Lone Christians do not survive long: we need the Church as much as the Church needs us.

It is vital to realise that whatever the problems of a church, being part of a larger community is vital. The followers of Jesus were made to belong with others. It is not just that we grow best in community; it is also that we were not meant to walk the way alone.

23

ESSENTIAL 5:
DEVELOPING THE CHARACTER THAT GOD WANTS

The fifth essential principle involved with walking with God centres on character. Here, though, we need to pause for a moment to think of what 'character' means because the term has lost a lot of its significance today. To talk about someone's character used to refer to what, deep down inside, they were like in terms of moral values. Character was important because it controlled what you were and how you acted: it gave rise to your behaviour. So, faced with temptation, someone with a good character would choose what was right while someone with a bad character would choose what was wrong.

Today, however, 'character' often means just 'personality', as in when we say that someone has 'a pleasant character'. The nearest thing to the old idea of character is that of *integrity*. To have 'integrity' is for your public life to match your private life; you never say one thing and do another. The idea of 'integrity' is weaker than that of 'character' because it doesn't take account of God's standards but, nevertheless, it is a start.

However, the older idea of character needs recovering. For one thing, it is found throughout the Bible. It is easy to think that the Bible is just about behaving in the right way but in fact it is concerned with developing the sort of character that gives rise to right behaviour. Jesus made this clear: 'A good tree can't produce bad fruit, and a bad tree can't produce good fruit. A tree is identified by its fruit. Figs are never gathered from thorn bushes, and grapes are not picked from bramble bushes. A good person produces good things from the treasury of a good heart, and an evil person produces evil things from the treasury of an evil heart. What you say flows from what is in your heart' (Luke 6:43–45). In fact, much of the teaching of the New Testament, in particular, is about developing the character God wants.

So if this is the character that God wants of us, how do we obtain it? The phrase from Micah that we have followed throughout this book – to act justly and to love kindness and to walk humbly with your God – is again helpful here. But this time, let's start with the last thing that is mentioned in it – the need to walk humbly with God.

We have thought about how we walk with God in terms of two stages. The first stage is conversion: that drastic, one-off change where we let God's presence and power into our lives. Without this fundamental change, we can never walk with God at all. Yet conversion is just the first step and to walk with God takes more than just one step.

The second stage is the life-long companionship with God as we walk along the road of life and it is this long-term walk with him that develops our character.

How does it work? Well, suppose that, for a year, you had the opportunity to work closely with a great man or woman, morning to evening, day after day. Almost certainly, you would be changed by being with them. You would probably find that you picked up their way of thinking, their values, maybe even some mannerisms. The same principle, only more so, applies with God. Spend time with God and you will discover that you change. Walk the road of life with Jesus and something of who he is will inevitably rub off on you.

Two things are important here. The first is that the walking *humbly* aspect shouldn't be overlooked – if you want to learn from someone else, humility is the best attitude to have. We need to come to Jesus as a learner, not as a critic. The second is that character formation takes time. The tree of character that produces the fruit that God desires grows slowly and requires frequent care and attention. No quick-fix solution exists for acquiring the character that God wants us to have. A saying makes the point: 'Character is not made in a crisis, it is only exhibited.'

How do we develop the character that God wants? The answer is to walk with God, not just to let God's characteristics rub off on us but to deliberately and purposely seek to imitate who he is. The apostle Paul gave a good rule to the followers of Jesus at Ephesus: 'Imitate God, therefore, in everything you do, because you are his dear children' (Ephesians 5:1). At the heart of our journeying with God there should be this plea: 'Lord, make me more like you. Through your Spirit shape me so that, deep down, I increasingly have the character of Jesus.'

What would that character look like? Here, too, we return to familiar ground in our answer. It is to have right attitudes and to do right actions.

First, God wants a character that has *right attitudes.* When people walk closely with God they come to see the world from his perspective. The result is that – increasingly – their viewpoint on life is that of God himself and their attitudes and their character change. And as their character changes, so, in turn, does their behaviour. They become those whose deepest desire is to show love, mercy and faithfulness to others. They come – in Micah's phrase – to 'love kindness'.

Second, God wants a character that produces *right actions*. The real importance of character lies in the fact that it produces our actions. Those who walk with God are people who do not simply have the right attitudes – they carry out right actions too. Indeed, one of the marks of having the sort of character that God desires is that there is no gap between attitude and action. Those who walk closely with God are not content to simply shake their heads over some tale of misfortune or injustice: they get out and do what they can to remedy it. Their love is not just words: it is seen in their acts of kindness, mercy and faithfulness. In short, they *act justly.*

We started this book with God's challenge through Micah for right actions and right attitudes and then moved on to look at how we needed to walk with God. Now – after thinking about who God is and how we walk with him – we are back with right actions and attitudes. Yet everything has changed. Those who walk closely with God and let him change them will find that they begin to fulfil what he commands. We perhaps thought, as many do, that 'to act justly and to love kindness and to walk humbly with your God' meant that by doing right actions – which is hard – and having right attitudes – which is harder! – we might *possibly* get to walk with God. In fact, we see that the reverse is true – it is only by walking with God that we will get the new Christ-like character that makes us want to have right attitudes and to do right actions. Doing what is right may still be hard work but it is now what we want to do. God has changed our desires. Right actions have gone from being a burden into a delight.

In many ways, this would make a good end point for this book. We have returned – hopefully somewhat wiser than when we started – to where we began. We have found that while God has demanded right actions and right attitudes from us, he has also given us the means to fulfil those demands. Through Jesus Christ, he has come alongside us on the way of life so that, if we choose, we can be changed into people who have right attitudes and want to do right actions. God has turned 'acting justly and loving kindness' from being a *prescription* of what he requires of us to being a *description* of what we actually desire for ourselves. Yet, rather than stop here it is worth looking ahead. For all of us, the road of life stretches on ahead for an unknown time. There is still some distance to travel and some guidance needs to be given on walking the road to the end.

24

THE **WAY AHEAD**

In this final chapter, we need to look at travelling the road ahead. The key to continuing to walk successfully with God is having the right outlook on the three dimensions of life – the past, the present and the future.

1. LOOKING BACK: HAVING THE RIGHT OUTLOOK ON THE PAST

You might think that people would have few problems with the past – after all, it no longer exists except as a memory. Yet many people are troubled by the past – some try to avoid their past because it is so full of regrets, hurts and guilt while others find themselves stuck there, trapped by recriminations or grief. Neither reaction is healthy. The first sort of person can end up throwing away the good of the past along with the bad, the second is unable to move on. Yet how can the past be healed?

Here, the Christian is helped because Jesus can help us 'get past the past'. Forgiveness and guilt are key issues. How do you ask forgiveness of someone with whom you have lost contact? How can you experience forgiveness if someone who refused to forgive you has died? One of the remarkable features of Jesus' teaching in the Bible is that he claims to offer forgiveness, not just for wrong things done against himself, but also those done against others (see Mark 2:10; Luke 7:48). It is one of those claims that only makes sense if Jesus is God.

For almost two thousand years, the followers of Jesus have found in him forgiveness for what happened in the past. Yet the healing Jesus offers goes beyond giving people forgiveness. It also extends to giving the power to forgive to those who need it. The Holy Spirit has enabled the followers of Jesus to grant forgiveness in situations where forgiveness seemed impossible. In other cases where the past hurts – perhaps where it is a source of grief, disappointment or a sense of failure – the testimony of Christians is that Jesus can bring healing. Yes, the scars of the past may remain, but the wounds themselves have healed.

One reason why it is important to have a past without wounds is because our experience of the past can be a source of great help to us in walking the way of life with God. First, the past can stimulate us to be grateful to God. Looking back, we can identify situations where God blessed us (perhaps in giving us friends, prosperity or health) or where he had mercy on us (perhaps in protecting us from the consequences of our actions). Second, the past can give us warnings. Looking back, we can see where our weaknesses lie and can take action to prevent a repetition of trouble. The saying that 'Those who forget the past are condemned to repeat it' doesn't just apply to nations. Finally, the past can bring us encouragement – when we look back and see the difficulties that God has brought us through, the future may not seem so daunting.

2. PRESSING ON: HAVING THE RIGHT OUTLOOK ON THE PRESENT

Followers of Jesus possess the privilege of having their past healed. Yet the fact is that our task is to live in the present. The following guidelines should help us to have the right outlook.

Walk with God day by day. It is surprisingly hard to live in the present without the future threatening us. Some people look at the challenges that walking with God presents and become intimidated by what lies ahead. 'I will never be able to do that,' they say of some looming difficulty, and get discouraged. The secret, as in any other human venture, is to take things one day at a time. In the Lord's Prayer we are told to ask for 'our daily bread': to pray for what we need on a day-by-day basis. Every single day of our lives, we need to make a deliberate effort to walk with God. If we follow God on that basis, we will soon be surprised at how far we have come.

Distinguish between feeling and fact. The followers of Jesus down through the ages have reported how at times God has seemed distant or even totally absent. Sometimes these feelings are easy to explain: the person concerned has either drifted away from God or has let something come between them and him. Yet people who have apparently been following God closely have also spoken of times when he has seemed silent. One partial answer is that these are apparent absences rather than real ones and that God allows them so that we come to rely on faith and not on our feelings. There are times when we need to remember that the basis of our relationship with God is not our feelings, but the fact that we have entered into a covenant relationship with him. A pilot may often have to fly a plane without seeing the ground. There are times – thankfully, mostly of short duration – when walking with God can be like this. Don't panic, but keep going in faith!

Never postpone what must be done. The future holds a further danger: it can tempt us to postpone doing what we have to do. So, for example, we can fool ourselves into dreaming how, one day, we will get things right in our life and *then* walk properly with God; in the meantime, though, we will do nothing. It is on this basis that many people delay committing themselves to Christ or postpone doing what they know God wants them to do. 'I will do it tomorrow,' they say, but all too soon there is no tomorrow. It is a good rule to do immediately what needs to be done.

Work at walking with God. Walking through life with God is a little like walking up a down escalator. Pause, however briefly, and you will soon find yourself falling behind. We need to keep up with God – to read the Bible regularly, pray, have fellowship with other followers of Jesus and keep worshipping him. The Christian life is a bit like riding a bicycle – the one guaranteed way of falling off is to stop.

Don't expect the way to get easier. You might expect that, with time, walking with God would get easier. It would seem only fair that, after all our efforts, we might finally make it to some smooth, flat stretch where we can take our ease. The reality is otherwise – while there are downhill moments on the way of life, they are generally only long enough for us to get our breath back. Like the good parent that he is, God delights in stretching his children to their limits. There are always new challenges, new things to learn and new issues to face. And when you hit a slow patch, remember that God guides our stops as well as our steps.

Be careful of shortcuts. On any long walk shortcuts are tempting and walking with God is no different. Shortcuts appear in many forms: perhaps as a quick-fix remedy to becoming holy or as an instant solution to unleashing God's power in your life. The desire to find a shortcut is understandable. For one thing, those who seek such shortcuts are often commendably troubled by their own lack of spiritual progress. For another, God *can* do sudden, wonderful and liberating acts in his children's lives and sometimes he does just that. Yet it is a wise comment that there are no shortcuts to anywhere worth going. Certainly, the only map of the way – the Bible – knows nothing of any shortcuts. Most of the time, to walk with God involves making slow and steady progress, one step at a time. The road ahead is a straight road, even if it is narrow. Abraham Lincoln observed that no one ever got lost on a straight road. He might have added that there are also no shortcuts on a straight road.

Seek companions on the way. The wisdom of company on the way is something that we have looked at, but it need not apply only to a church fellowship. Indeed, even within a fellowship there is wisdom in having close friends with whom you can share your problems and challenges.

Watch your step. There is no state of human existence that doesn't have its own temptations. Prosperity can breed complacency, joy can produce carelessness and trouble can generate despair. What is the answer? We need to stay honest with ourselves and to watch our lives carefully, anxious lest we slip away from walking closely with God. Micah's great question and answer should continuously challenge us. Do we act justly? Do we love kindness? Are we indeed walking humbly with our God?

Don't be discouraged. There will be times when something distracts us and we find that we are no longer walking with God. There are two possible responses. The disastrous reaction is to tell ourselves that we have totally failed, get thoroughly discouraged and give up. The sensible one is to turn, as fast as we can, back to God. Trying times are not the times to stop trying.

A final thought on having the right attitude to today: 'Yesterday is a memory; tomorrow is a mystery. Today is a gift from God and that is why we call it the *present*.'

3. LOOKING FORWARD: HAVING THE RIGHT OUTLOOK ON THE FUTURE

The third and final dimension of walking with God is the future. There is a strange paradox in how human beings look at the future. People delight in looking forward and are always thinking about what they will do next weekend or on their holidays. Yet they have a very selective view of the future – the most distant prospect most people will dare to think about is retirement. The unavoidable fact of death is rarely considered.

Yet those who walk with God can look at death with confidence – they know that Jesus has defeated this most fearsome of enemies. Those who do not walk with God have no such hope: they can only turn away from death. If we have come to God and learned to walk with him, we need have no fear that, when it comes to the hardest part of the way, he will leave us.

There is a story of how, when a missionary talked to an old Native American chief about Jesus, he told him how Jesus was the only way to eternal life. After he had finished, the chief responded, 'The Jesus road is a good road. But I have followed my people's road all my life and I cannot change now.' A year later, the old chief was dying and the missionary hurried to his side. The chief turned to him and asked, 'Can I turn to Jesus now? My own road stops here. It has no way through the valley.' The Bible teaches that not only does 'the Jesus road' lead on through that dark valley into a sunlit eternity beyond but Jesus will not leave us as we travel through the valley. We do not know what is in the future but we know the one who holds the future. That is far better. When followers of Jesus talk about death, three words are used a lot – victory, glory and certainty.

Victory. Throughout the New Testament, death is treated as a defeated enemy. Jesus brought people back from the dead, rose from the dead himself and promised that his followers would rise from the dead. Paul summarises what this means in the following words, 'Then, when our dying bodies have been transformed into bodies that will never die, this Scripture will be fulfilled: "Death is swallowed up in victory"' (1 Corinthians 15:54). Of course, along with this sense of triumph there is realism: Christianity does not hide the fact that death persists as an ugly, painful and tragic fact. Yet, for followers of Jesus, it has lost its final chilling power. Death does not mark the end of life but instead the beginning of real life – the grave is an entrance, not an exit.

Glory. When most people today think – if they ever do – of the afterlife, they generally think of the dead surviving in the form of disembodied spirits, beings who have become shadows of what they once were. However, this is not the message of the Bible. The teaching there is plain – those who know Jesus will be raised from the dead, will be given very real and glorious physical bodies and will live forever in a restored world that is free from sin, sorrow and suffering. The future state the Bible portrays is one of such splendour, substance and reality that it is our lives now that will seem like shadows. While we may not understand all the details, the Bible is plain – the future for God's children is glorious.

Certainty. The New Testament declares that, on a day unknown to us, God will, without warning, end history and raise the dead. This awesome view of the future is confidently assumed. This confidence arises from Jesus' own resurrection from the dead, an event showing not only that he is master over death but that death's long cruel reign will end. In Revelation 1:5 Jesus is described as 'the faithful witness to these things, the first to rise from the dead' and one day all his brothers and sisters will follow him out of death's control. While God does not promise his children a comfortable journey, he does guarantee a safe landing.

Yet, the Bible is plain that such a hope belongs only to those who have chosen to follow Christ. Throughout the Bible, the message is that there is only one way that leads to life. Jesus himself warned his contemporaries, 'Enter through the narrow gate. For wide is the gate and broad is the road that leads to destruction, and many enter through it. But small is the gate and narrow the road that leads to life, and only a few find it' (Matthew 7:13–14, NIV). This is the bottom line – of all the many ways that human beings can travel, only one leads to eternal life.

The Christian hope of the eternal future, of being with God forever and of being permanently free from all those things that trouble us, is the greatest encouragement there is to keep on walking with God. Life for those who know God and who walk with him is not a purposeless exercise: we have both a companion and a destination. One day, we will go round some corner of the way and realise that, at last, we have come to the end of this life's road. In the glorious light of God's presence, we will see that he has brought us safely home.

APPENDIX

Details of the Ten Commandments DVD series and information about J.John can be found on the Philo Trust website, www.philotrust.com or from the following address:

Philo Trust
141 Witton House
Lower Road
Chorleywood
Rickmansworth
Hertfordshire
WD3 5LB
UK

OTHER BOOKS BY J.JOHN

Ten

Imagine a world where love guides every action. A community where people place others before themselves. A place where God is recognised and respected.

Thousands of years ago, God revealed the framework for life as it should be. Simple values for daily living that provide the foundations of our laws and principles. Yet society is slowly moving from this essential guide, as these absolute truths give way to a subjective culture. How can we reclaim these timeless truths for living and apply them in a modern world?

The Happiness Secret

It's something we all want, but what is happiness, and where can we find it?

In this thoughtful and uplifting book, inspirational speaker J.John takes a look at the most famous teachings of Jesus – the Beatitudes – finding clues to help us embrace a life of joy and fulfilment. He unpacks each of Jesus' great sayings, placing them in their first-century context and also reveals how they are applicable in our lives today. Ultimately, he suggests that if we seek happiness directly we may never find it; but if instead we seek a life of fulfilment we will find true and lasting happiness.

Accessible and down-to-earth, *The Happiness Secret* is a practical guide to attaining fulfilment and meaning in life as well as the perfect inspirational read.

The Life

There is no denying the importance of Jesus Christ in the history of humankind. He has walked through the last two thousand years of history, of empires, governments, political systems and philosophies and has remained as a dominant, challenging, yet mysterious presence.

In *The Life: A Portrait of Jesus* J.John and Chris Walley achieve an uncommon blend – a serious book for popular use and a popular book for serious reading.

The Return

Everyone knows the story of the prodigal son – or do they?

In this fascinating book, skilled communicators J.John and Chris Walley give a new twist to an old story. *The Return* is a three-part exploration of this most loved parable, combining fiction, Bible study and real-life testimony to open up this timeless story and its themes of grace and reconciliation.

To order please visit: www.philotrust.com